Your Opinion Doesn't Matter!

It's Your Customer's Opinion That Counts

Andrew Ballard

MarketingAtlas Publishing

"Ballard is right on...*your opinion doesn't matter*, unless you want to be your only customer. The steps are easy to follow, and made a mammoth difference in my business!"

—*Rod Watson, CEO, Prevention MD*

"It makes no difference whether you are a profit or not-for-profit organization, the principles in this book are crucial to succeeding in today's tough market. *Your Opinion Doesn't Matter* is factual and fun...a great read."

—*Carl Zapora, CEO, United Way of Snohomish County*

"As a small business owner every move and strategy must be effective to succeed. Andrew's system has helped us understand and identify an effective market strategy that we can actually implement. ROI is a 10!"

—*Ron Kirkendorfer, CEO, Northline Energy*

"Finally, an approach that's easy to understand and implement. This is a great book and a quick read. Every business owner needs to do the Northstar exercise."

—*Michael Kostov, Executive Producer, Kostov Productions*

"I have firsthand experience with Mr. Ballard's process. Based on my 25 plus years in advertising and promotion, I can say with confidence his system is the most effective I've ever used. Andrew's book does an outstanding job of detailing a step by step approach toward growing any business, regardless of industry."

—*Pete Talbott, CEO, The Talbott Group*

"Nobody I know has a better handle on how to research, plan and develop marketing strategy than Andrew Ballard. This book is a must read for anyone responsible for marketing their product or service."

—Travis Snider, President, BETS Consulting

"With our oversaturated market it is more difficult now than ever to generate a positive return, especially in the medical field. It takes solid customer perception data. That's what this book is all about, how to make marketing decisions based on the customers' point of view."

—Jerry N. Mixon, M.D., Founder, Longevity Medical Clinic

"Andrew truly appreciates the importance of connecting with customers and shares this vision in a step-by-step process that if followed has the real potential of enhancing business revenues."

—Cathy Reines, President & CEO, First Heritage Bank

"Andrew's advice continues to work extremely well. We have significantly increased our sale and market share. Through exit interviews, we are able to track sales each month that are solely due to strategies detailed in his book."

—Tim O'Neill, Owner, O'Neill's Wheels

Bulk discounts are available for education, business premiums
and not-for-profits. For bulk orders or permission please contact:

MarketingAtlas Publishing
914 164th Street SE #400
Mill Creek, WA 98012
Toll free: 1-866-843-2852
Email: Info@MarketingAtlasPublishing.com

Library of Congress Control Number: 2010911754

ISBN 978-0-9790042-0-9
1. Business   2. Marketing

Your Opinion Doesn't Matter: It's Your Customer's Opinion
That Counts
Author: Andrew Ballard – First Edition
Editor: Beverly Theunis

Printed in the United States of America.

10 9 8 7 6 5 4 3 2 1 0

Dedication

To Sandra: my wife, my best friend, and an amazing collaborator. Her tireless love and encouragement— and her self-effacing wisdom—remind me every day that there is a greater purpose than my own.

Acknowledgments

The system detailed in this book is about developing growth strategies that are based on the voice of your customer. In that spirit, I have practiced what I preach by gathering a test reader group to evaluate and voice their opinions about this book. My test readers were: Pete Talbott, Theresa Poalucci, Travis Snider, Deb Anderson, Cathy Feole, Peter Harvey, Louise Stanton-Masten, Cindy Rattray, Ed Lopit, Anna Simmons, and Greg Noren. I appreciate and value their contributions greatly.

Equally, I want to express my appreciation for the hundreds of clients who have allowed me to partner with them to position and promote their brands.

One such person, (a client and close friend) who has supported my work for many years, is Pete Talbott, Managing General Partner of The Talbott Group. Pete was an early adopter of my system, and he continues to advocate customer research as the ally, not the enemy, of advertising agencies. Pete "gets it."

Rarely does anyone achieve success in a vocation without the guidance of someone who has gone before and paved the path. For me, Don Schultz, Professor Emeritus of Service at Northwestern University, is that person. Renowned in the international marketing community, he is considered the "father of integrated marketing communications". Don has given me great counsel regarding this book, and I am grateful for his support.

Another person I want to thank wholeheartedly is a colleague, a friend, and my editor, Beverly Theunis. Simply put, I could not have done this without her. Beverly burned the midnight oil on many occasions, and helped me get through this labor of love. I thank Beverly for her writing talent, her coaching, and her patience.

Finally, I want to acknowledge the most important person in my life, my wife Sandra. She helped me write this book by doing a considerable amount of research and planning. She is also my business partner and a companion research nerd. She deserves a gold medal just for putting up with me for 20-plus years, and for working on this book with me for the past seven of those years. It has been a long journey, and without her love and encouragement, I probably would have not finished.

Foreword

Don Schultz, Ph.D.,
Professor Emeritus-in-Service,
Integrated Marketing Communications,
Medill School of Journalism, Northwestern University

Doing The Right Things, Right

There's an old saying, "It's more important to do the right things than to do things right". In other words, being precise in what you do is of little value if you are doing the wrong things.

But, quite honestly, to be successful, you have to do both. And, that's what makes this book unique. It's about how to do the right things in sales, marketing and managing your business. And, it's a guidebook on how to do them the right way. That's the winning combination Andrew lays out so well in this text.

This marketing book really is unique. It's a text devoted to, for and about small businesses. Businesses too many authors and experts have overlooked. Yet, small businesses are still the backbone of the U.S. economy. They just haven't been treated that way.

But, in this text, small business people get the attention they deserve, in a book crafted by a communications expert who has specialized in working with and for small businesses most of his career.

Running a small business is a tough job. Too many things to do. Too many alternatives. Too much information on some things, not enough on others. That's particularly true in marketing and marketing communications. There are so many new things, it's easy to get caught up in the excitement of web sites, Facebook, Twitter and all the new gadgets and gizmos. And, even the old traditional media communication forms have changed. They've gone "digital"…digital newspapers, digital radio, digital in-store signage and all the rest. With so many new promotional forms and fashions, you could spend most of your day simply trying to keep up. Not running the store, just watching what is going on outside the store…in the marketplace.

That's why, when Andrew first contacted me about this text, *Your Opinion Doesn't Matter*, I thought, here comes another author with stars in his eyes and promotional concepts running rampant in his head.

But, that's where I was wrong. And, that's why I agreed to write the foreward to this text. It has a message I believe in…strongly. And, it has been written by a self-made entrepreneur who has learned the lessons of the marketplace through experimentation, trial-and-error, but, mostly by observing what customers do and don't do. Because it is the customer that makes up the marketplace. The customer is the key ingredient for the small businessperson and entrepreneur. That's where you succeed or fail, and, let's face it, you can't afford to fail very often if you're operating with your own money. Work for a big company and you can fail dozens of times simply because they have deep pockets. My suspicion is, if you are reading this text, it's because it is "your money" that is on the line, not some faceless investor, or an impersonal banker or maybe even the government.

A Major Difference In Marketing Approaches

If you've ever picked up a marketing text, you've probably noticed the first thing the authors discuss is the product or service they are trying to sell. They urge you to study the product, know it inside out, find the differences between your product and your competitors. Immerse yourself in product knowledge.

That's the old, industrially-based approach to marketing.

Andrew starts with the right focus. The one that really generates success. He starts with the customer. The person you want as a supporter of your business. That's the reason for the title of the book, *Your Opinion Doesn't Matter…It's Your Customer's Opinion That Counts.* And, he's absolutely correct. What you think. How you feel. What you want to accomplish. None of it matters. It's what customers care about that will drive your business…higher up to the next level or down to the bargain basement where few things have any value and those that do, don't keep that value very long.

So, Andrew starts with customers. Because customers are the only ones with money. Your store or shop has no money. Your plant or factory has no money. Your suppliers have no money. Only customers have money. And, your job as a businessperson is to get more of those customers to give you more of their money for longer periods of time. That's really what marketing is or should be about. Building relationships with customers that increase your cash flow and increase their satisfaction with their lives.

Customers have money. Nothing else does.

It's All Process

In this book, Andrew provides you with a process. A way to think and a way to do. It starts with customers, but, then it progresses through eight key steps. Follow those steps, in the order in which Andrew presents them, and you'll be on your way to success. But, that sounds so lock-step doesn't it. Following a formula. A straight and narrow path. Just the reason you didn't pursue the corporate pathway in your career.

But, I can assure you, the process works. For one thing, it gives you a way to think about marketing. A way to evaluate alternatives. Or, as Andrew says "A Northstar" that guides and directs you. That "Northstar" concept is critical to your success. If you don't know where you are going, any roadway will take you there. If you have a clear understanding of what your business is, what you are trying to achieve, what you want to accomplish and know what kinds of customers will help you get there, you've made the biggest decision since you decided to start your own business.

It's all about process and it's all about structure that will help you navigate the rough waters of small business.

It's More About Listening Than Talking

Too many marketing, advertising and promotional books are all about "talking". What you want to say to customers and prospects. Marketing has always been about talking. Telling customers what we think they need to know. Listing the reasons you should do business with us or our company. Shouting from the rooftops. And, likely turning more people off with our shouting than bringing them in with offers and values on things they really want or need.

That's the "old marketing".

The "new marketing", which Andrew advocates, and I endorse, starts with listening. Listening to customers. Asking them questions. Getting their opinion, even if it differs from yours. Finding out what they want or need or would like to have.

And, once you've listened, responding. Filling their wants, needs and desires through the products and services they have told you they'd like to have.

Today's marketplace is based on filling consumer needs. Not selling. Need filling. It has a fancy name if you want to use it... Demand-Generating Marketing. But, it simply means doing what Andrew advocates in this text. First, listening to customers. And then, responding. He calls it "Voice of the Customer" but once you've tried it, you'll call it brilliant.

And, by listening to customers first, you'll find you'll save a heap of money on marketing. Listening helps you become more effective with your marketing programs, not just be more efficient with your spend. And, you'll learn the first law of new marketing...spending less should be the real goal of marketing. Too long, we've envied marketing organizations that have spent tons of money to sell a car or a tube of toothpaste or a box of macaroni. Those are old marketers.

The new marketers are folks like Apple who didn't spend very much to promote the iPhone and, even less to merchandise the iPad. Yet, everyone wanted one and most of them paid full price to get one. That's the real value of marketing. Adding, not subtracting, value from a product or service.

But, enough of my views.

I truly believe Andrew has a strong message for all small business owners.

Most of what you need to develop marketing and promotion into a profit center for your business is in this book and the accompanying work sheets Andrew has developed.

Read the book. Use the worksheets. But, most of all, take the time to listen to customers. It's their opinion that counts, not yours. That's what is really new in marketing today. It's the customer, not the product that really matters. Learn that lesson and you'll be on your way to greater success.

Marketing IQ Test

Evaluate each of the following eight questions objectively. Rate your performance for each on a scale of 0 to 10. Add up your ratings and enter the total score in the bottom box.

Key: 0 = Nonexistent, 10 = Masterful.
A perfect score would be 80.

1   **Northstar:** Do you publish and adhere to a mission statement for your business? ☐

2   **Business Analysis:** Do you review the strengths and weaknesses of your business frequently? ☐

3   **Customer Research:** Do you interview your customers to learn about their opinions? ☐

4   **Competitor Comparison:** Do you study your competitors for their strengths and weaknesses? ☐

5   **Market Niche:** Do you have a profile of your most responsive and profitable market segment? ☐

6   **Market Position:** Do you have a competitive distinction valued by your market niche? ☐

7   **Promotion Alignment:** Do you have a marketing communications plan aligned to your position? ☐

8   **Optimal Results:** Do you have a tracking system to regularly evaluate/enhance marketing tactics? ☐

Total Score ☐

How to Use this Book

Since you are reading this book, most likely you have ambition and responsibility, a self-regulating combination.

Ambition is a state-of-mind or a value that gives you purpose and the drive to set and accomplish your goals. Responsibility is a position you've earned and keeps you accountable for achieving your goals.

This book is intended to help you focus your ambition and responsibility upon the activities of business development (marketing and sales) in ways that can produce optimal results for the growth of your business.

The eight questions in the Marketing IQ Test on the previous page correspond to the eight steps of the system detailed throughout this book. If you skipped doing that test, please go back and do it now.

For any questions that you rate yourself less than four, you should spend extra time studying their corresponding chapters.

Marketing IQ Test Score Classifications:

Score	Classification
71 - 80	Marketing Genius
61 - 70	Marketing Executive
51 - 60	Marketing Director
41 - 50	Marketing Manager
31 - 40	Marketing Coordinator
21 - 30	Marketing Intern
11 - 20	Marketing Student
0 - 10	Marketing Novice

If you scored over 70, put this book down and go teach a class!

I have written this book in simple terms, avoided as much industry jargon and techno-babble as possible, and explained the industry terms used. You don't need to be a "marketing genius" to understand and apply the concepts in this book. And if you have a marketing background, the system will likely focus your activities and improve your results.

Step-by-step, and using real world examples, I demonstrate how to define and promote your *market position*, based on the *voice of your customer*. As you follow along, you will see how this system melds the process of strategic planning with the practice of marketing.

Finally, each of the eight steps includes highlighted tips and illustrations, and concludes with exercise summaries and example worksheets (included in a companion Workbook). These straightforward exercises will help you in applying each step of the system.

Tip: You will get the most out of this book by first reading it all the way through without stopping to do the exercises. Then go back through it again, and use the exercises as a step-by-step guide for applying the system to your business.

"The discipline of writing something down is the first step toward making it happen."

Lee Iacocca,
Retired President & CEO,
Chrysler Corporation

Documentation is a critical success factor in any strategic process. After completing all the exercises, organize them sequentially, and you'll have a plan convenient to reference as you go about the work of growing your business.

You can also conduct any of these eight exercises individually, if you have a specific need or purpose. But to keep balance in your business, it is best to conduct all eight exercises in sequence.

Introduction

"The more you engage with customers
the clearer things become and the easier it is
to determine what you should be doing."

John Russell,
Former Managing Director, Harley-Davidson Europe

Unless you'd like to write a check for buying back your own inventory, *your opinion doesn't matter.* Understanding and using the "voice of your customer" can accelerate and sustain your growth curve because *it's your customer's opinion that counts.*

But how do you learn and act upon what your customers really think? This book was written to demonstrate how to accomplish this by using our Market Analysis Positioning System™, which we are proud to introduce in these pages (referred to throughout as "MAP System" or "MAPS"). You will be shown how a market analysis (that helps you understand your customer and competitor dynamics) leads to defining and promoting a distinctive market position. The MAP System in this book is research-based and is the foundation for creating and validating effective strategy.

My Personal Background

From a very young age I had a marketing intuition. Whether it was my first lemonade stand or selling door-to-door as a Boy

Scout, I just knew instinctually how to connect with the customer and move product.

Growing up, my hero was Peter Drucker (the undisputed management guru of the 20th Century). My favorite Drucker quote is, "The purpose of business is not to create a product; the purpose of business is to create a customer."

(When I was a teenager in the '70s, most of my friends hung posters of Farrah Fawcett, one of the stars in the TV show, "Charlie's Angels." Me? I had a framed picture of Peter Drucker!)

Perhaps it's because both my parents were in the advertising business. I admit that I'm a bit obsessive, maybe even anal-retentive when it comes to marketing. (My wife is convinced that I was potty trained at gun point.)

Early in my career, when moving up to the national advertising scene, I had a smart boss who gave me some sound advice. He told me that for each client situation I'd have to choose between a few paths. He said, "When you come to a fork in the road, talk to me before making a decision because I'm the million dollar man." That sounded a bit arrogant to me. My facial expression must have tipped him off because he immediately followed with, "No, you don't understand, that's how much I cost the company last year by screwing up."

He was telling me that I could learn from his mistakes. In turn, after 30-plus years of successes and failures, now I can help you avoid many of the conventional marketing pitfalls, and show you how to incorporate a proven approach toward growing your business.

The genesis of the *your opinion doesn't matter* concept began many years ago when a client shared a story, a story that changed my perspective. I am now a growth strategist, but at that time I was a marketing consultant. The story goes like this.

A shepherd was tending a vast flock of sheep alongside a country road. A brand new Lexus SUV came screeching to a halt in front of the shepherd. A young man saunters out of the vehicle. He was wearing an Armani suit, a Cartier watch and Gucci sunglasses. As he approached the shepherd he said, "If I can guess exactly how many sheep you have, can I have one?" The shepherd looked out over acres and acres of sheep, looked back at the young man and said, "Alright."

So the young man walks back to his SUV and pulls out a razor thin laptop and a mini satellite uplink. He logged in to the GPS system of the NASA website, and pulled down 60 spreadsheets filled with algorithms. A minute later he printed out a 150-page report from his wireless printer. As he was thumbing to the last page, he walked back to the shepherd saying, "You have 1,531 sheep!" Somewhat stunned, the shepherd said, "You are correct, take your prize."

The young man walked out to the center of the field and picked up the biggest animal he could find. As he was stuffing it in the back of his Lexus SUV, the shepherd approached him and asked, "If I can guess your profession, will you pay me back in kind?" The young man said, "Sure, I have nothing to lose." The shepherd said, "You are a consultant." The young man looked dejected and said, "How did you know?" The shepherd replied, "First, you came without being called. Second, you charged me a fee to tell me something I already knew. Third, you don't know anything about my business. And, I would really like to have my dog back!"

I realized at that moment in time, if this is how my clients viewed "consultants", then I needed to reposition myself. And that was the first time I realized, *my opinion doesn't matter.*

Smarts and Supply Aren't Enough

To thrive in today's competitive and volatile marketplace, you should set your own preferences and perceptions aside, and focus on what your customers care about. In a supply and demand driven market economy, the preferences and perceptions of your customers regarding your products, people and services can make or break your business.

Bankruptcy courts have been filled with smart business owners and entrepreneurs who had good ideas and products. According to the Small Business Administration (SBA), only 34 percent of employer firms survive 10 years. My hunch is that the survival rate is much lower for non-employer startups (one-person businesses). My point is that the odds of surviving are stacked against small businesses. The Map System in this book, if properly applied, will help change the odds in your favor. And if you have passed the 10-year milestone, congratulations! However, you wouldn't be reading this book if you were fully satisfied with your rate of growth.

Moral: it takes more than *smarts and supply* to be successful long-term. It is vital that your growth strategies are based on the *demand* side of the marketing equation.

Definition of Marketing

Marketing is somewhat of an abstract term in how it means different things to different people, depending on their professional perspectives. To a brand manager, it means establishing a distinctive identity and maintaining a positive image. A marketing director would likely define marketing as the activities related to generating awareness and leads. A sales manager might contend that marketing is about identifying, qualifying and converting prospects into customers. And they are all correct.

Most business owners, however, don't care how you define marketing. They just want more money coming in than going out, and on a regular basis.

I have had the pleasure of working with hundreds of small business owners and, regarding running their businesses, the number one complaint I hear is "managing cash flow."

Poor or inconsistent cash flow is often the result of ineffective marketing.

Webster's definition of marketing, in part, is "...all business activity involved in transferring goods and services from producer to consumer." If you accept that definition, as I do, then everything you do in your business should be in support of marketing. Because until you sell something to somebody, you won't have cash flow.

Following is a superb definition of marketing.

"Authentic marketing is not the art of selling what you make but knowing what to make. It is the art of identifying and understanding customer needs and creating solutions that deliver satisfaction to the customers, profits to the producers and benefits for the stakeholders."

Philip Kotler,
Professor of International Marketing,
Kellogg School of Management

To Kotler's revealing quote I would like to add my belief that effective marketing is the result of both *science* and *art*, in that order.

Keys to Success

To succeed in today's cluttered and competitive marketplace, you need to do four things effectively.

☞ *Define your niche* by subdividing the larger market into smaller segments, and then target those that are most responsive to your offerings and profitable to your business.

☞ *Shape your position* to be meaningful and memorable. In other words, your market position needs to be distinctive in your industry and valued by your target market.

☞ *Align your promotion* in support of your market position so your target market will clearly understand how you can best solve their problem or satisfy their need.

☞ *Optimize your results* by pre-testing your message and tracking the effects of your promotion so you can make informed adjustments to improve your return on investment.

Those keys to success are the _last_ four steps in the MAP System. The _first_ four steps lay the foundation for success. The system you are about to learn isn't rocket science, nor does it require excessive time or exceptional marketing know-how on your part. It is a research-based approach that gets results because the structure is in place for your use to analyze the market and to develop growth strategies—based on your customers' opinions.

I have developed hundreds of growth programs—using this system—for small and midsize businesses. It's a proven process that works well in any industry and market.

The key to success is to define and promote a distinctive market position based on the voice of your customer.

Following is a model of the Market Analysis Positioning System™. It is intend to demonstrate the process flow of the eight steps that follow this introduction. While the model may appear complex, the system is not difficult to understand and apply.

MAPS Model

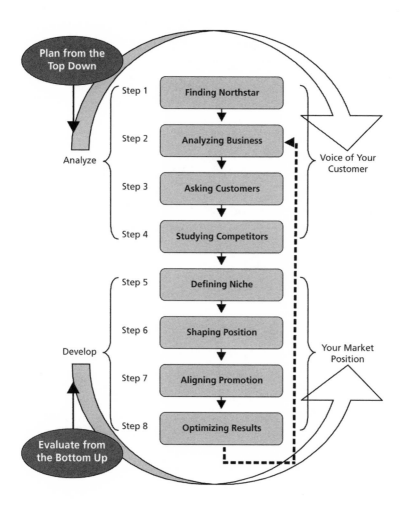

Finding Your Northstar

"You've got to have some Northstar you're aiming for, and
you just believe somehow you'll get there…"

Steve Case,
Cofounder, America Online (AOL)

In preparation for writing this book I surveyed nearly 1,000 small business owners. I found that fewer than 10 percent of them had a mission statement that was documented and published.

Also, among those companies with a published mission statement, I found that most of their employees (internal customers) didn't know what it was.

A mission statement is a company's Northstar, a guiding light to keep your business on course. My favorite Yogi Berra saying is, "If you don't know where you are going, you might wind up someplace else."

The purpose of a mission statement is communicating who you are, what you do, and whom you serve—to both internal and external customers. Your internal customers (employees, stakeholders, suppliers, partners, etc.) are just as important to the success of your enterprise as your external customers. If your own people don't "get it" they won't be able "give it!"

The mission statement is also a good decision-making tool, and should be the litmus test for everything you do. When you have an opportunity to consider, or an important decision to make, run it through your mission statement. If the idea or opportunity under consideration doesn't support your mission, it should be discarded.

> "Singleness of purpose is one of the
> chief essentials for success in life, no
> matter what may be one's aim."
>
> *John D. Rockefeller,*
> *Founder of Standard Oil Company*

Your mission statement is the Northstar of your business and should guide your growth strategies. Without a Northstar, it is more difficult to develop an effective market position.

The Good, the Bad and the Ugly

No, this isn't a tribute to spaghetti westerns; rather, here are a few examples from Fortune 500 companies to illustrate the rights and wrongs of mission statements.

The Good

"To organize the world's information and make it universally accessible and useful."

Google's mission statement is short and to the point. This is a mission you might actually remember. The only reason it is good instead of great is that it doesn't identify who they are (by name).

The Bad

"FedEx will produce superior financial returns for shareowners by providing high value-added supply chain, transportation, business and related information services through focused operating companies. Customer requirements will be met in the highest quality manner appropriate to each market segment served. FedEx will strive to develop mutually rewarding relationships with its employees, partners and suppliers. Safety will be the first consideration in all operations. Corporate activities will be conducted to the highest ethical and professional standards."

I use this example as "bad" because, at 75 words, it is unlikely to be remembered by an employee, let alone a customer or a stockholder. Although FedEx refers to this as a "mission" on their website, it reads more like the opening of a keynote address at an Annual Meeting.

The Ugly

"Apple designs Macs, the best personal computers in the world, along with OS X, iLife, iWork, and professional software. Apple leads the digital music revolution with its iPods and iTunes online store. Apple reinvented the mobile phone with its revolutionary iPhone and App Store, and has recently introduced its magical iPad which is defining the future of mobile media and computing devices."

The above statement is displayed on the Investor Relations' FAQ page of Apple's website. To me, it reads like copy for a TV commercial written by someone "under the influence."

Okay, so I'm a David slinging at a Goliath. But I'm not the only one poking fun at Apple for their mission statement. The Blogosphere is full of comments and jabs.

And I'm not impugning the integrity of these highly successful companies. These examples are just to show that even megabrands do make mistakes when it comes to crafting a mission statement. (Of course, that isn't a license for you to do it!)

Mission Statement Exercise

Writing an effective mission statement, this first step in the MAP System, involves a simple three-step process: 1) answer three questions, 2) select key information, and 3) write the statement. This will only take about an hour, and should involve other key people (employees and stakeholders if you have them).

Step 1: Answer Three Questions

Write words and phrases that answer each of the following three questions: 1) who you are, 2) what you do, and 3) whom you serve.

Your written answers don't need to read well or even be justifiable at this point.

The only objective of this first step is sketching descriptive information. The fine-tuning process will come later.

Who you are: Define who you are by writing your company name and its business category or industry. The reason your company name must be included in your statement is that you will publish your mission in most of your marketing communications. Toward that end, don't lead off with: "Our mission is..." Rather, start off with your company name. If your company name doesn't describe what business you're in, indicate your industry also. For example: US Bank's name identifies their industry, Wells Fargo's does not. If your company is not as well known as Wells Fargo, you should add the industry in your mission statement to clarify your product category.

What you do: After you've described who you are, write what you do in factual terms. It's important to bear in mind that prospective customers view experts and specialists offering niche products or services as more appealing than generalists. Example: US Bank specializes in SBA lending.

Whom you serve: The third question addresses your target market. Write down the customer group(s) you are (or will be) marketing to. Example: SBA lending for small businesses expanding or making capital improvements.

Step 2: Select Key Information

Go back over your answers to all three questions in Step 1 and select the key information by marking (underline or circle) the words and phrases in each answer that you feel should be included in your mission statement. Then put all the selected key words and phrases together in one paragraph.

This paragraph might not make sense...it doesn't have to at this point in the exercise. The only objective of this second step is to identify, select and consolidate the most important information. Be sure to have your customer's hat on while deciding what words or phrases to select.

Tip: Doing this exercise on a flip chart or whiteboard will facilitate group participation. Allowing everyone involved to watch the progression of work is highly beneficial.

Step 3: Write the Statement

After you've put your key information together, you're ready to write a concise statement in one short paragraph. Begin drafting your statement by arranging the key information in logical order. Then create a coherent flow with appropriate punctuation and grammar. You (and your team if you have one) will rewrite your draft statement a few times until its final form is satisfying.

In "finding your Northstar" (crafting your mission statement), it doesn't matter what order the information is presented, as long as it answers all three (who, what and whom) questions. When you get close to a final draft, be sure to read it out loud. A statement that sounds good aloud will read better.

Tip: If you rewrite your statement more than six times, you might be getting too picky. Laboring excessively over a word or phrase probably won't amount to making a difference in the customer's mind.

Some years ago, I was facilitating a board through this exercise when a heated discussion ensued between two directors over a single word. They might have been too close to the trees to see the forest, or had a bit too much caffeine during the retreat. In any case, they wasted time and didn't add value to the process or final outcome. My advice is that you don't let your ego or a personal agenda get in the way. After all is said and done, *it's your customer's opinion that counts.*

Two Rules

I have two ironclad rules for any mission statement: 1) it should be 25 words or less, and 2) it must communicate a customer benefit. The reason for the "25 words" rule is two-fold. First, it will force you to focus on the key points that are most relevant to your customer and, secondly, a short statement is far more apt to be read and remembered—nobody is likely to read or remember a mission "dissertation".

> "If a person can tell me the idea in 25 words or less, it's going to make a pretty good movie."
>
> *Steven Spielberg,*
> *Academy Award-Winning*
> *Film Director and Producer*

I hope the reason behind the inclusion of a customer benefit is obvious. After all, this entire system is focused on a demand orientation. Your mission statement must be easy to understand and relevant to your customers' wants, needs, and desires.

Following are a few examples of mission statements that meet all the criteria of a well-constructed mission statement through 1) explaining who they are, 2) stating what they do, and 3) whom they service, and including a customer benefit—all in 25 words or less.

"The Anheuser Busch mission is to be the world's beer company, enrich and entertain a global audience and deliver superior returns to our shareholders."

"Graybar is the vital link in the supply chain, adding value with efficient and cost-effective service and solutions for our customers and our suppliers."

"As a full-service agency, Marketing Solutions develops and implements research-based growth strategies that help small businesses accelerate their sales and share."

Completing the simple three-step exercise above will make it much easier to find your Northstar. Once you find it, continually use it to stay on course.

Tip: It is a good idea to run your final draft past a few key customers. If you are a startup, show it to a few associates and vendors. Remember, unless you're going to buy back all your own inventory, *your opinion doesn't matter.* It's very important to understand the customer's point-of-view.

Step 1 Exercise Summary:

In a group setting, develop your mission statement by following this three-step process.

1 Answer the questions of who you are, what you do, and whom you serve.

2 Select the key words and phrases important to communicate, and put them all together in one paragraph.

3 Using your key words, write and rewrite a mission statement (not more than 25 words and with a customer benefit) until you are satisfied with a final version.

Mission Statement

Write a short descriptive paragraph for each of the first three categories below. Circle the best
key words or phrases that define the mission you want to convey and use them in your draft.

☞   **Who We Are** (company name, industry or product category, values):

_____

_____

☞   **What We Do** (products/services, the purpose of business):

_____

_____

☞   **Whom We Serve** (the individuals or customer groups to be targeted):

_____

_____

☞   **Statement Draft** (List your circled words/phases in a logical order, then write your draft):

_____

_____

_____

_____

_____

_____

Analyzing Your Business

"Think as you work, for in the final analysis, your worth
to your company comes not only in solving problems,
but also in anticipating them."

Harold Wallace Ross,
Creator of the New Yorker Magazine

Anticipating opportunities and challenges is a very important part of developing effective growth strategies. It involves analyzing your *internal business situation* and *external market environment*. This process is referred to as a Situation Analysis or SWOT Analysis (*Strengths, Weaknesses, Opportunities* and *Threats*).

The purpose of conducting a SWOT analysis is to determine the internal and external conditions that may have an impact on your business.

Strengths and weaknesses are internal (company) conditions within your control. Opportunities and threats are external (market) conditions outside of your control. The objective is to take advantage of your strengths and opportunities and deal with your weaknesses and threats.

Assessing these *company* and *market* conditions will help you anticipate scenarios and plan the most appropriate actions. Steven Covey, author of *The 7 Habits of Highly Effective People* preaches, "Sharpen the saw," as his seventh habit. If you don't take stock of your weak points, you won't know what needs sharpening.

> "You don't hear things that are bad
> about your company unless you ask. It
> is easy to hear good tidings, but you
> have to scratch to get the bad news."
>
> *Thomas J. Watson, Jr.,*
> *Founder of IBM*

If you have staff, you absolutely must involve them in your SWOT analysis. *Their opinion counts* because they are customers— your "internal" customers. When it comes to gathering "head out of the sand" information about your company's current situation and market environment, front line employees can give you the straight dope...if they don't fear reprisal. (I have facilitated many SWOT exercises with only top level executives participating; those reports read more like an autobiography...amusing but not always accurate.) Give your people a safe place to participate with "no fault honesty."

Internal Conditions

You'll begin your SWOT analysis by identifying internal company conditions, which are either strengths or weaknesses, based on your current situation, that is, where you are today—not where you want to be tomorrow.

It is possible for any condition to show up on both your strengths and weaknesses lists. For example, "sales" may be on the strengths list (because they are increasing) while also showing up on the weaknesses list (because your sales force lacks accountability and their activities are fragmented).

From a strengths standpoint, you might think, "We're OK because sales are increasing." However, that identified weakness shows that you should also be concerned about sales you're losing because of inadequate organization, tools or support.

Strengths and Weaknesses Primers

Because you are developing marketing and growth strategies, look at (but don't limit yourself to) the traditional marketing mix as primers, also known as the 4-Ps of marketing: *product, price, place* and *promotion.*

☞ **Product:** the goods and services offered by your business. In terms of innovation, quality and competitive advantage, what are the strengths and weaknesses of your products and services? Among your portfolio, which are the profitability contributors or detractors?

☞ **Price:** the cost, fees and pricing strategy you incorporate to transact business. How do your prices stack up against the competition? Do they support your market position? Remember that price without consideration of value delivered doesn't paint the whole picture.

☞ **Placement:** the location, distribution and delivery system of the goods and services you offer. Does your distribution strategy create a competitive advantage, or disadvantage? Is there anything about your location, logistics or delivery system that can be leveraged or should be improved upon?

☞ **Promotion:** the communication actions taken to develop awareness and interest, such as advertising, public relations, sales promotion, and personal selling. Are you doing anything that distinguishes your brand? Are you lacking a positive return on promotion investment?

Your marketing mix is the best place to start your business analysis and generate a conversation around your strengths and weaknesses.

Other primers include your company's infrastructure, such as *facility, finance, people,* and *technology.* Look at everything that either helps or hinders your ability to market and sell your products and services.

☞ **Facility:** the plant, physical location or store front of your business. Is your current facility sufficient to advance your enterprise or is it holding you back? Consider both functionality and aesthetics (especially if customers come on site).

☞ **Finance:** the available capital, cash flow situation, and financial management practices of your business. Do you have an adequate reserve? Are you leveraging your assets? Is the budget aligned in support of your marketing objectives?

☞ **People:** all of the people employed and contracted by your company. Do you have good organizational alignment, or are there areas that can be improved. Having the right people in the right places, or not, can be a game changer.

☞ **Technology:** the information and communications technology, as well as the equipment owned or leased by your company. What are the costs/benefits of upgrading your technology? Are you pacing with, ahead of, or falling behind your industry or competitors?

External Conditions

You may question the rationale for taking time to catalogue external conditions that you cannot control, such as political, social, and economic events. But the fact is, although you may not be able to control external conditions, you can and should respond to them.

Unlike the internal analysis, which concentrates on present day circumstances, an external analysis should consider both current and forecasted conditions—but not for more than a few years out.

With the economy, for instance, there are advance indicators, e.g., gross domestic product, that forewarn of a slowing or accelerating economy several months before small businesses and consumers experience its impact. Other leading indicators include building permits, T-bill rates, and the money supply. Keep track of the leading indicators that have the greatest impact on your industry.

By noting such advance indicators, you can make strategic decisions that will help you weather economic storms—such as holding more capital in reserve as opposed to making investments that may take a long time before bearing fruit.

Before the down economy of 2001 came to a crest, I recommended to one of my clients that they hold off on investing in a new product line they were eager to launch. Having the extra cash reserve enabled them to take market share from key competitors who couldn't afford to promote themselves during the economic downturn. Consequently, my client's "share of voice" increased significantly and an increase in "share of market" soon followed.

Tip: It is usually easier to take market share from competitors during a down economy than a boom cycle—if you maintained the necessary reserves to continue your promotion while your competitors are pulling back.

Opportunities and Threats Primers

In terms of external opportunities and threats—market conditions beyond your control—there are four primer categories you should assess: *customer*, *consumer*, *competitor* and *industry*.

☞ **Customer:** how the buying behaviors and satisfaction levels of your customers are affecting your business. It's important to know if your customers are buying more or less based on past behaviors. Keeping your finger on the pulse of your existing customers is fundamental to retaining them.

☞ **Consumer:** how consumers in general (not your customers) are buying products or services in your industry. Are there any trends emerging that may either help or hurt your business? Are there any shifts in demand? Are any new wants and needs surfacing?

☞ **Competitor:** how the extent to which competitor actions or situations could impact your business. Knowing what your key competitors are doing, in terms of their marketing mixes (product, price, place and promotion), will help you seize opportunities and mitigate threats.

☞ **Industry:** how any industry trends or changes could impact your marketing and sales efforts. Is there anything on the horizon within your industry that you need to be mindful of as you plan your growth strategies?

Tip: Don't confuse strategy and opportunity. The distinction between the two is that a strategy is controllable and an opportunity is not. For example, to target communications toward an emerging market segment is a strategy. The opportunity would be stated, "There is an emerging market segment that may value our product."

In addition to making an assessment of customer, consumer, competitor and industry conditions, conducting a PEST analysis is an effective way of exposing potential opportunities and threats. The PEST acronym stands for *Political, Economic, Social* and *Technology*.

☞ **Political:** this includes administrative, legislative, judicial and regulatory conditions (including taxation) that have the potential of helping or hurting your business. This is an especially important area to keep your eye on if you play in a heavily regulated space.

☞ **Economic:** the local, regional and national (even global depending on your market) economies and how they impact your industry. Do you know which economic indicators are most important to your business? Some industries actually benefit from a down economy...where are you positioned?

☞ **Social:** any social or cultural trends that may have an impact on your product category. Currently, a relatively new condition added to the social list of external conditions to watch is terrorism. Look at how the 9/11 attacks significantly increased American Flag sales, and at the same time, devastated the airline industry. What are the social conditions that may present opportunities or threats to your industry or business?

☞ **Technology:** innovation and technological advances may be constructive or destructive to the way you operate. This is more of an issue now than ever before. Look how the advent of micro processing put the kibosh on typewriter sales, and how that same technology spawned the personal computer industry.

A tale of two companies: Smith Corona was one of the market share leaders in the typewriter industry for decades, but they didn't account for advances in technology in their business plans. They sued for bankruptcy protection in 1995. By then IBM, another manufacturer of typewriters, had introduced the IBM PC (in 1981), the PCs and their clones were representing 91 percent market share in the personal computer category, and the company was number seven on the Fortune 500 list.

These are merely thought starters for using the MAP System and not intended to limit your thinking. By objectively assessing which internal and external conditions affect your business, you'll be well prepared to begin developing your four SWOT category lists.

SWOT Analysis Exercise

Using a flip chart, white board, or computer screen (projected so everyone involved in the exercise can see the work), begin the process of building a list in each of the four SWOT categories. The exercise involves a three-step process: 1) list SWOT conditions, 2) prioritize SWOT lists, and 3) determine SWOT actions.

Step 1: List SWOT Conditions

Begin your SWOT exercise by listing your most important company strengths. These should be major company strengths, not lesser strengths. During this first step you are not trying to prioritize, the order doesn't make a difference at this stage of the exercise.

After listing your strengths, list your weaknesses using the same process. After you finish your internal (*Strengths* and *Weaknesses*) lists, move on to your external (*Opportunities* and *Threats*) lists.

Tip: Limit yourself to 10 items in each of the four SWOT categories. This will force you to focus on the most important (or major) conditions. This is a maximum not a minimum. If you can't come up with 10 conditions on any or all four lists, that's OK.

Step 2: Prioritize SWOT Lists

When it comes to the to-do list, there is always more work than there is time. I liken small business owners to fire hydrants—we're either putting out fires or watching out for the big dog. No matter how good you are at multi-tasking, prioritization will help you to focus on the SWOT conditions most important to your business.

Start by prioritizing the items on each of your four lists. A simple way to prioritize a list in a group setting is to use sticky dots…those little adhesive dots you can buy at any office supply store. You can even number the dots.

After everyone has had a chance to vote, tally the dots on each of your four SWOT lists.

Next, on all your prioritized lists determine if each condition is actionable or not. Ask yourself, "Can I take action to capitalize on a strength or opportunity, or deal with a weakness or threat?" Notate all of the "actionable" conditions.

Once you have finished prioritizing the conditions in each of the four SWOT categories, and have determined which of them are actionable, you'll be ready to further condense your lists and then assign actions to your top priorities.

Step 3: Determine SWOT Actions

Begin by examining the actionable conditions on both your strengths and opportunities lists. Decide which of these would have the most significant effect on your business, and list the top two or three in an *actionable assets* priority list.

Go through the same process with your weaknesses and threats lists to determine your top two or three *actionable liabilities.*

It doesn't matter whether your top two or three assets are strengths, opportunities or a combination thereof. The same holds true when prioritizing liabilities. The point is to list the most important conditions you should capitalize on or deal with.

Large companies, with more resources at their disposal, may want expansive asset and liability priority lists. Small companies and individuals should keep their SWOT action lists short. It is far better to do a few things well than many things mediocre.

After you've completed the SWOT actions lists (one for your assets and one for your liabilities), document what action should be taken under each item listed. That will complete the exercise.

Assets (Strengths and Opportunities)

1. List the top priority and actionable strength or op-
    portunity
    Action: Enter the action you will take to capitalize
    on the asset
2. List the second priority and actionable strength
    or opportunity
    Action: Enter the action you will take to capitalize
    on the asset

Liabilities (Weaknesses and Threats)

1. List the top priority and actionable weakness or
    threat
    Action: Enter the action you will take to mitigate
    the liability
2. List the second priority and actionable weakness
    or threat
    Action: Enter the action you will take to mitigate
    the liability

Put your SWOT analysis results aside for now. You will use them in Step 6.

Step 2 Exercise Summary:

In a group setting, catalogue the internal and external conditions that may have the greatest impact on your business by following this three-step process:

1   Create four lists of up to ten strength, weakness, opportunity, and threat conditions.

2   Prioritize the items in each list and determine where to focus your attention.

3   Recap the top actionable priorities under asset and liability lists, and the actions you'll take for each.

SWOT Analysis

List the top 10 major internal conditions (Strengths and Weaknesses) and external conditions (Opportunities and Threats) that can have the greatest impact on your business.

Internal   External

Assets

P	Strengths	A	P	Opportunities	A

Liabilities

P	Weaknesses	A	P	Threats	A

Identify the most significant internal and external conditions related to your marketing success. Prioritize them in the P column, and if actionable, check mark them in the A column.

Asking Your Customers

"We slip from our obligation to know what consumers
are thinking...into believing they are like us; and from
there we slide further into believing we can think for
them and understand their actions."

William McComb,
CEO, Liz Claiborne, Inc.

This step is literally the foundation of my assertion that *your
opinion doesn't matter,* and of MAPS. At its core is the fact that most
small businesses make strategic decisions without asking customers
for their opinions. Knowing what your customers care about, and
what they don't care about, should be the driver of every major
decision you make.

Voice of the Customer

Collecting the "Voice of the Customer" (VOC) is a popular research technique that involves interviewing customers to better understand their preferences, perceptions and experiences. This is a
proven process that facilitates improvement of product development,
marketing communications, and customer services. It is also a powerful approach to defining your market position, and distinguishing
yourself from competitors.

There are many benefits of asking your customers for their opinions. Acting on VOC data can improve the results of promotion and customer acquisition activities, increase customer retention, and generate more referrals. Also, knowing how your customers experience your products, people and services can enable quality and process improvements. Process improvements usually produce happier customers and higher profits.

The big brands have been doing this type of research for decades. Some auto manufactures hire agencies to deliver new models to car reviewers, typically reporters and feature writers. They do this not only to gain press coverage, but also to collect voice of the customer data.

A friend of mine is the publisher of a newspaper, and she has been reviewing new cars for many years. She told me that reviewers have access to what is being written by other reviewers, and that many of the write-ups point to the same problems, such as soft brakes or road noise. She noticed that when she reviews the same car model a year later, she finds that these problems have been fixed. The manufacturers pay attention to what reviewers write about and make product improvements accordingly.

(My publisher friend also told me that her neighbors think she's a drug runner because she's had a different new car parked in her driveway each week for the past 17 years.)

The bottom line is that, when effectively incorporated, VOC data can accelerate the growth of your business.

Understanding the preferences and perceptions of your customers (or target market if you are a startup) is critical for your business to succeed and grow. Remember, unless you intend on buying back all of your own inventory, *your opinion doesn't matter.* In the practice of marketing and growing your business, *it's your customer's opinion that counts.*

A fundamental principle of marketing is that, "The customer is always right." You may already know the two rules of customer service:

☞ **Rule #1,** the customer is always right;

☞ **Rule #2,** when the customer is wrong, refer back to rule #1.

After all, proving your customers wrong won't make you right, it will only make you broke. Even when customers are wrong, their beliefs (perceptions) still drive their attitudes and behavior.

In many cases, customers have misperceptions about companies and product offerings. Customer misperceptions are more common in the early stages of the life cycle for a product or service, however, the chance of customer perceptions not lining up with your business reality can happen at any stage. It's an axiom of marketing psychology that, "People do not react to reality, they react to their perceptions of reality." This trait of human nature is why it is so important to understand how your customers perceive your product and service offerings.

Marketing research has tiers of complexity. A study, and the data collected, is only as valid and reliable as the methodology used and how it was executed. That said, the purpose of this book is to avoid the complex and present a simple "how to" approach.

VOC Exercise

A basic VOC study involves a four-step process: 1) choose collection method, 2) select your sample, 3) develop a questionnaire, and 4) analyze the data.

Step 1: Choose Collection Method

This first step involves deciding how to go about collecting voice of your customer information. There are many methods, including point-of-sale, telephone, online (email and website surveys), mail and packaging (response card).

Many researchers use quantitative (large sample) methods, such as opinion polls and satisfaction surveys, which are effective at aggregating large amounts of data with statistical accuracy. The method I'm suggesting is qualitative (small sample) through *in-depth interviews* and *focus groups*. I prefer these approaches because they allow for a conversation with customers, and the ability to probe for underlying motives and values.

Since you will be collecting the voice of *your* customer, you have access to the population you want to study; therefore, recruiting VOC participants should not be difficult.

If you produce or deliver a product, or are in a service sector, you have direct contact with your customers and can invite them to participate in an interview or focus group. If you're in retail, and don't have customer contact information, you can recruit participants at the point-of-sale (via clerk or cash register).

In-Depth Interviews

In-Depth Interviews (IDI) are one-on-one interviews, either in person or on the phone, that are designed to dig deeper than traditional surveys, and to uncover underlying motives and values that drive an individual's decisions and behaviors.

Most often, we use IDIs to collect VOC data because it is easier to schedule individual interviews than scheduling several people for a focus group. That is especially true when your customers are all over the country. In-depth interviews also allow collection of more details about a participant's desires, opinions, and experiences concerning the company or product being evaluated. Such details not only help grow your business, they can also uncover flaws in planned products, and demand levels for them. Here's an example.

Many years ago we conducted an IDI project for a human resources company planning to launch a new product. After 25 interviews it was clear that it would have failed to gain any traction in the marketplace. At the end of our debriefing session, and as he was signing our check, the CEO said, "This is the best money I've spent in some time." I responded, "You have a healthy attitude." He replied, "You just saved me $2,000,000." Our motto is "test before you invest", and IDIs are a great way to do just that.

An in-depth interview normally takes 30 minutes or more, but we have found that a good deal of VOC information can be collected in a 15-minute interview using a well-structured questionnaire. As long as the study objective is specific, you can ask (and probe) 8 to 10 topics, and reduce the risk of participant "burn out".

Focus Groups

A focus group, also referred to as a Focus Interest Group (FIG), is typically used for gathering consumer reaction to a new product concept, weigh product and service attributes, and test advertising elements (messages and images). We've even used FIGs for optimizing websites to increase click-through and conversion rates. Focus groups are a great method for collecting voice of your customer data and delving into customer experiences and attitudes. They are also effective for brainstorming (solving product or promotion problems) and painstorming (solving customer frustrations).

Focus groups involve pre-qualifying a small group of individuals for collecting their feedback on specific topics. Consumer FIGs, sessions of two hours, are best on weekday evenings and late Saturday mornings, and food and beverages should always be served. Business FIGs are limited to 90-minutes on a weekday with lunch served.

Tip: For both consumer and business FIGs, avoid Monday and Friday as attendance won't be high. Proximity is another critical success factor for filling a FIG since most people won't travel far to attend.

Registering participants is easy compared to enticing them into actually showing up. Usually incentives are necessary, but even with cash incentives no show rates can be as high as 30 percent.

Products and services can be used for focus group incentives. As an example, Microsoft incentivizes with software typically valued at several hundred dollars.

The value of the incentive depends on the market you are targeting. For instance, a series of FIGs with high school seniors that we did for a community college took only $20 and free pizza. Nearly everyone showed and would have hung out with us all day if we wanted. On the flip side, a FIG we conducted recently with a group of business banking customers was incentivized with $150 and free lunch, but barely bought us 90 minutes with only 70 percent attendance.

We usually conduct focus groups in sets of three for every project, market segment, or market location. But if the budget does not permit three, one is infinitely better than none at all. Our smaller clients glean great insights from a single focus group.

It is important that facilitators keep a focus group on track. It is the facilitator's job to also mitigate any dysfunctional group dynamics arising from conversation monopolizing, or from asserting judgment on others' opinions. It is OK for participants to disagree, but not be disagreeable. You've heard the saying, "One bad apple can spoil the bunch." It's true of both fruit and focus groups.

Where should you hold your focus group(s)? Anonymity is so important to collecting candid and unbiased data that your place of business is not an option.

If you want to avoid the cost of a focus group facility, a hotel meeting room can be an ideal FIG venue. Some hotels will reduce the room fee or eliminate it if a modest banquet is ordered.

Tip: Ask the hotel to set up your space "boardroom" style, so that all participants can see each other. Sit the facilitator at one end of the table with no chair at the other end. Also, make sure every participant signs to acknowledge receiving their incentive.

Whether to do in-depth interviews or focus groups, or a combination of both, depends on your VOC objectives and your customer base.

Focus groups are best if you want group interaction, people feeding off each other's comments, and the use of visual aids. In-depth interviews are a better choice if you have an upper income customer base, customers who are not centrally located, or a need for more detailed or intimate information.

Step 2: Select Your Sample

A sample is a small representative group of the overall population being studied. A small subset of your entire customer base is queried to gain insights into your customer base beliefs.

Random samples are queried for most kinds of consumer studies and opinion polls. But in collecting voice of your customer data for making strategic decisions on how to best position and promote your product or brand, I suggest you query a sample of your best customers. Understanding the values and attitudes of your most responsive and profitable customers will give you the most lucrative insights. If you include opinions from your less desirable customers in optimizing your marketing mix, you risk attracting less profitable customers.

However, you can learn even more compelling information from customers you have lost.

> "Your most unhappy customers are your
> greatest source of learning."
>
> *Bill Gates,*
> *Chairman, Microsoft*

Lost customers can help you pinpoint the problems and weaknesses that lead to customer attrition. While collecting opinions from them is more challenging, their information is generally more actionable. You will hear "no" more often when asking them to participate in IDIs (usually FIGs are not a good approach), but I promise you this: your extra effort will be worth it.

Include only customers lost in the past year since recollections from more than a year ago are unlikely to be accurate or relevant to your current business situation.

In-depth interviews and focus groups are qualitative studies, which are small in sample size and not held to the same statistical standards as large sample quantitative studies.

Sample sizes are variable and depend on the size of your customer base. For studies using IDIs, a sample can range between 10 and 50 participants; we usually aim for 25 whenever possible. However, for a new insurance company (with few customers) I once conducted IDIs using only 10 participants, which resulted in a couple dominant themes that were very directional and proved one of their primary business assumptions wrong. This small sample of VOC data made a huge difference in the company's direction.

For conducting focus groups, between 8 and 12 participants is ideal. Keep in mind that, based on the strength of the incentive offered, you likely will need to over-recruit participants to achieve this sample size (remember you'll have no shows).

Another important principle of sampling is segmenting. It is important for the sample to be drawn from customers of a single market segment, product or service. For example, the consumer and business customers of a bank would not be mixed in the same sample.

In research speak we call this a "homogeneous segment" meaning that they are all the same. If you have two different segments you want to study, they will require separate VOC samples.

When screening to recruit qualified participants, exclude anyone working in the industry being evaluated or in the advertising and marketing business.

Regardless of the size or number of your customer base, your market segments or product lines, *your opinion doesn't matter.* Go with a small sampling of customer opinions rather than no data at all. A small sample can serve you well if you ask the right people: those you want to replicate!

Tip: To collect candid and unbiased VOC data, participant anonymity is crucial. It's OK if you and company stakeholders (the study sponsors) know who participated in your sample. However, never attribute specific comments to individuals by name. In fact, it is best to have an outside expert facilitate collection and reporting.

Step 3: Develop a Questionnaire

Asking the right people (your sample) addresses only half the voice of your customer equation; asking the right questions is the other half. The design of your questionnaire will have a big impact on the usefulness of the information you collect.

A questionnaire for determining the most valued selling features or product attributes, and why, would be quite different from one that delves into customer service experiences, or one meant for a painstorming exercise. So, begin designing your questionnaire by deciding your objective—what you want to accomplish and how you will use the information.

In planning traditional studies, researchers develop a "problem statement" for bringing an objective into focus. Be clear and specific on the objective and how you will act on your VOC data.

Once you have your VOC objective documented, use it as a guide for creating an appropriate questionnaire. Designed to serve more as a guide, it should be less structured than a questionnaire for a traditional survey. With a survey you ask a question, document the response and move on to the next question. But the VOC process for in-depth interviews and focus groups involves a back and forth conversation on each topic. So after the initial response to a question, you dig deeper by probing.

Probe with questions such as: Will you give me an example? Can you elaborate on that point? How did that make you feel? What changes or improvements would you recommend?

Questions for researching the voice of your customer are open-ended, requiring an explanation versus a yes or no response. The goal is to get the individual or group talking, not deciding. An effective series of open-ended questions involves the "*keep, stop, start*" sequence.

☞ **Keep:** Questions that elicit what about your customer's experience is most appreciated or valued, what they love about your product, service or doing business with your company. In other words, what they would like you to *keep doing.*

☞ **Stop:** Questions that let you learn what about your customer's experience is frustrating for them, what they
would like to see changed or improved, what they don't
like and could cause them to switch to another provider.
In other words, what they would like you to *stop doing.*

☞ **Start:** Questions that help you understand what your
customers are missing, or what you don't provide that
they want and could send them to a competitor for that
product, service or specific feature. In other words, what
they would like you to *start doing.*

Another useful question we usually ask is, "What is the single
most important deciding factor when choosing a brand (provider,
product, or service)?" And we always follow up that question with
"why?" In VOC research, "why" is just as important as "what".

Other practical questions include, "Who do you consider the
greatest competitor" and "What media do you use most often" (favorite radio station, TV program, newspaper or magazine, websites,
social media, for example). If our client advertises, we also ask their
customers how they initially found our client to determine which
advertising channels are most effective.

These are the kind of common and useful questions you might
use, but the basis of your questionnaire should be from your industry and information that you can act upon for improving the
experience of your customers. In developing your questionnaire (in
the form of a guide), focus on your VOC objective and keep the
number of questions to a manageable number. If you are having
trouble limiting your list of questions, your objective may not be
specific enough. Don't try to solve all of your problems, or guide
several marketing initiatives, with one study. There should be only
one objective per study.

Setting the stage before you begin questioning participants is
very important to having a productive FIG or IDI. Make sure participants understand the study objective, why they have been selected,

and how long the session will last. For a focus group, you would also give guidelines on constructive group interaction.

Before conducting the study, always test your questionnaire with a few customers to make sure of clarity in concepts and proper sequencing of questions. Using simple and common language works best, and sequencing your questions properly will ensure that no question will bias responses to questions that follow.

Step 4: Analyze the Data

After you've acquired your VOC data (asked the right people the right questions), you can tabulate, analyze and act on the information you've collected. The first step of tabulating (organizing) is entering the responses into a spreadsheet, using one column for each question. Each row represents the response of each participant.

ID#	Q-1	Q-2	Q-3	Q-4	Q-5	Q-6
R1						
R2						
R3						
R4						
R5						

Key: R = Respondent, Q = Question

After all the responses have been entered, go through them one at a time for each question and group similar responses into categories. Not every response will fit into a category, but natural patterns and themes will emerge from this process. (Armed with the most dominate themes that surface for each question, you will be clear what actions will produce the greatest impact, from the customer's perspective.)

Next, prioritize the categories based on the number of responses in each.

If you also collected VOC from lost customers, be sure to compare those results with your current customers, especially wherever frustrations, weaknesses and suggested improvements are apparent.

Tip: To collect unbiased and actionable VOC data, and to maintain the anonymity of participants, it is always best to work with a professional facilitator or interviewer. Collecting, analyzing and reporting on voice of your customer data require specific skills. Working with a pro will deliver the best results.

Put your VOC results aside, as you did with your SWOT results. We'll come back to them in Steps 6 and 7.

Step 3 Exercise Summary:

Develop and document your objectives for VOC research and follow this four-step process:

1   Determine the best VOC collection method, in-depth interviews or focus groups.

2   Recruit participants among your best customers and lost customers within a specific target market/product segment.

3   Design questions that are open-ended, and in a guide form to discover what your customer would keep, stop and start.

4   Tabulate all of the responses to organize your VOC information into logical categories, and then prioritize.

Voice of Your Customer

Based on your research objectives and customer base, determine which voice of your customer (VOC) collection method is most appropriate: In-Depth Interviews (IDI) or Focus Groups (FIG).

☞ Select Your Sample:
Because you want to replicate your best customers, profile and select the most appropriate customers and segments to participate in your IDI or FIG.

Profile current customers: those you want to replicate, by product or customer segment

_____

Profile lost customers: those you have lost in the past 12 months (to understand why)

_____

☞ Develop a Questionnaire:
To understand customer (and lost customer) experiences, preferences and perceptions, develop a questionnaire or guide to interview individuals or groups.
 – Keep: questions that determine what about their experience they value most
 – Stop: questions that determine what they would change or improve (frustrations)
 – Start: questions to determine what they would add to what you already offer

Other useful information to collect includes: most important deciding factors, greatest competitors and their favorite media. Frame your questions:

_____

☞ Analyze the Data:
Organize the responses from your IDI or FIG by grouping similar responses to each question into categories as a means of surfacing dominant themes you can take action on.
 – Enter responses into a spreadsheet: questions by column and respondents by row
 – Review each column of responses and group common responses for tabulation

Enter key findings:

_____

Document your key findings for future action on addressing customer experiences, preferences and perceptions. Set aside info on their most important values (keeps) for your work on Step 6.

Studying Your Competitors

"Nothing focuses the mind better than the constant sight of a competitor who wants to wipe you off the map."

Wayne Calloway,
Former CEO, PepsiCo

As important as collecting the voice of your customer is to the ultimate goal of growing your business, you also need information on your top competitors. Without knowing what they are doing (how they are positioning and promoting themselves) it would be nearly impossible to define a market position that is distinctive in your industry.

If I asked you, "Which of your competitors should you study?" and you try to answer that question before analyzing your VOC data, then you haven't fully bought into the MAPS premise. Remember, *it's your customer's opinion that counts.*

Tip: Always collect the voice of your customer before gathering competitive intelligence so you'll know which competitors to study.

In our client discovery process at the beginning of a new project, one of the questions we ask is, "Who are your top competitors?"

Sometimes the client is not certain, but even if they believe they know, we will be asking this question of their customers also, because *it's your customer's opinion that counts.*

When conducting interviews and focus groups, we always ask the participants, "If our client weren't in business, who would you likely patronize?" or some version of that question most appropriate to the industry.

It never ceases to amaze me how seldom our clients' list of top competitors aligns to their customers' list. But, finding these misalignments have also amazed my clients into realizing it's their *customer's opinion that counts.*

Some companies, especially not-for-profit organizations, don't want to come across as "competitive," which is understandable given the mission and values of some charitable organizations. However, most companies compete in a zero-sum economy. By that I mean one company's gain or loss is being balanced by the gains or losses of others competing for the same market. If you gain five percent market share it will likely come from your competitors, or vice versa. We all operate in a competitive marketplace. It doesn't matter whether you are a for-profit or non-profit business, you need to be competitively astute and adapt when necessary.

> "A competitive world offers two
> possibilities. You can lose. Or, if
> you want to win, you can change."
>
> *Lester Thurow,*
> *U.S. Economist and Bestselling Author*

Competitor Study Exercise

Conducting a competitor study involves a four-step process: 1) choose collection method, 2) identify top competitors, 3) collect appropriate information, and 4) organize the information.

Step 1: Choose Collection Method

There are several ways to collect competitor information including reviewing websites, blogs, social media, advertisements, collateral materials, and press coverage.

One of the tricks of the competitive intelligence trade is to set up a Google Alert on key competitors to monitor all of the new content (about their company) that hits the web. This is an effective technique for keeping track of news and press releases from your competitors.

But the *best* way to study (and experience) your top competitors is to "secret shop" them. This tactic involves a secret shopper posing as an interested prospect. Especially if you are in retail, physical (in-store) shops are best for monitoring your competitors.

Be sure to have secret shops conducted by someone other than yourself, if there is any chance you could be recognized. Another reason for having your shops conducted by outsiders is to have them leave a return phone number or email to see if the competitors shopped follow up with the prospect (secret shopper). It may be surprising, but in shops we've conducted (and we've done thousands), many small businesses do not follow up on prospect inquires. Some don't even ask for contact information.

If physical shops are not practical for your business or service industry, conduct phone shops. Start by putting together a plausible scenario for your secret shopper, followed by a short list of questions you want asked.

A secret shop scenario (that informs the shopper about their pretend situation and inquiry) helps ensure they won't get caught through stumbling or contradicting themselves when shopping the competitors.

In addition to asking the secret shop questions, have your shopper note observations such as the respondents' phone smile, product knowledge, how many rings before the phone call was answered, automated voice system or a live reception, whether they qualify the shopper, or ask for contact information.

Your shop scenario and guide will be based on your industry. Keep it short and don't allow anything in the scenario or questions be a tip off to competitors that they are being shopped. Another reason for using an outsider is that you don't want your business to be identified by a competitor's caller ID.

Step 2: Identify Top Competitors

From the voice of your customer data, review the responses to the "who is the greatest competitor" question. Compare your customers' lists to your list, and make an informed decision on which competitors to study.

It's possible your VOC data won't produce a definitive list of competitors. In that case, it would be up to you to select the most appropriate competitors to study. Questions to ask: Who is the competitor I am hearing about or losing business to most often? Who is closest to my location (if proximity is relevant)? Who is targeting my market segment? Who is the most aggressive at promoting their business? Who has the most market share?

Depending how cluttered or competitive your marketplace, you might study only the top three to five competitors. You don't need to study all of the competitors in your space, just those posing the biggest threats. If you have a regional or national footprint, you may need to study many competitors.

For the purposes of this exercise, focus on direct competitors.

Step 3: Collect Appropriate Information

After you have identified your top competitors, you'll want to study different aspects of their business and marketing. The most appropriate information to collect should be based on your industry and what its customers expect, the problems they are trying to solve, and needs they are trying to satisfy.

In the form of a study guide, list the information you want to collect on competitors, which may include (but not limited to):

☞   Target market focus
☞   Product or service focus
☞   Pricing and related policies

☞   Positioning strategy
☞   Promotional tactics
☞   Customer service policies
☞   Service area (footprint)
☞   Guarantees

Some information is more difficult to collect. For example, not all of your competitors may be clear on their positioning strategy. In our competitor studies we generally use this question in trying to extract that information: "We are deciding between your company and brand X (which is our client), why should we choose you over them?" In forcing your competitors to compare themselves to your business, this question also reveals what they are saying about you.

Best questions to ask are those that will help you understand your competitors' strengths and weaknesses relative to your business or product.

Step 4: Organize the Information

Rather than relying on your memory, document every competitor's answer to every shop question asked.

Incredibly, there are some business owners out there who don't document their information from their secret shops. I can't tell you how many times prospective clients have told me, "Yes, we did competitor research, I know what my competitors are doing." When I ask to see their documentation, the typical response is, "It's all up here," as they proudly tap their index finger to the side of their forehead. I then ask them, "What is your greatest advantage relative to your number one competitor's positioning strategy?" After a moment of silence I either get thrown out the door or become their new best friend. Again, don't rely on your memory!

Put all of the information collected into a spreadsheet so you can compare all your competitors. We developed a spreadsheet that compares our clients side by side with their competitors. In your spreadsheet, also, enter responses about your company (as if you were shopping yourself).

Characteristics	Your Company	Competitor 1	Competitor 2	Competitor 3
Target Market				
Product Focus				
Special Features				
Market Position				
Customer Service				

Key: Characteristics = the questions from your secret shop guide

This approach allows you to easily see everyone's strengths and weaknesses, and it will be very useful when shaping your position. Set this spreadsheet aside for Step 6.

Step 4 Exercise Summary:

Study your top competitors to understand their relative strengths and weaknesses by following this four-step process:

1   Choose the best secret shop method for your industry—physical (on-site) or phone shops.

2   Based on your experience and VOC data, identify the top competitors to shop (usually three or five).

3   Develop an industry appropriate shopper scenario and questionnaire to collect competitor information.

4   Enter the information collected into a spreadsheet and answer the same shop questions on your own business.

Competitor Study

In addition to reviewing online information (website, blogs, social media), determine which secret shop collection method is most appropriate: physical (in-store) shops or phone shops.

☞ **Identify Top Competitors:**
Based on how your customers answered the "greatest competitor" question in your VOC study, and on your list of top competitors, identify the top three to five competitors you want to shop.

1 _____   Location/Phone: _____

2 _____   Location/Phone: _____

3 _____   Location/Phone: _____

4 _____   Location/Phone: _____

5 _____   Location/Phone: _____

☞ **Collect Appropriate Information:**
Based on your industry and what is important to your target market, develop a secret shopper scenario (pretend prospect situation) and questionnaire based these thought starters:

- Target market focus
- Product or service focus
- Pricing and related policies
- Positioning strategy

- Promotional tactics
- Customer service policies
- Service area (footprint)
- Guarantee

Develop plausible shopper scenario:

_____

_____

_____

_____

☞ **Organize the Information:**
Enter all of your competitor responses to the shop questionnaire into a spreadsheet. Each row on the spreadsheet represents a response; and each column represents a competitor.

After you've set up a spreadsheet and all of the shop information has been entered (for reviewing in a side-by-side comparison of all competitors) put this information aside for Step 6.

Defining Your Niche

"We don't start out with the assumption
that our company is for everybody."

William McGowan,
Chairman, MCI (former phone company)

One of the most common mistakes that I see, especially among small businesses, is the attempt of appealing to a mass market, or one that is far too broad for their available resources. Some marketers assume that their product or service is for everyone; this mindset will land them in the category of businesses that fail. So, a critical success factor of asset allocation is to know where to aim your marketing resources.

The mistake of going after too broad a market is made because the function of targeting (narrowing your sights) seems counterintuitive. You would think that the larger net you cast, the more fish you'd catch. While that may work for fishing, it usually has the opposite effect for marketing, especially when marketing with very limited resources. After using MAPS, though, you'll know where to cast your net.

In fishing for customers with a limited marketing budget, you need to throw your net in a pond, not an ocean. By attempting to expand your market reach beyond your budget reach you would, in effect, fragment your budget and reduce the impact of your marketing resources.

Put another way, imagine if you took an eye dropper, and put a drop of ink into a five gallon bucket filled with water, swirl the water around, and what do you see? Nothing at all, the single drop of ink had no visible impact in the bucket of water. Now, take the same amount of ink and drop it into a one ounce shot glass filled with water, it turns the water dark. Big impact!

That same dilution principle applies to the marketplace. Fragmenting your budget over a large market won't get you noticed; however, if you concentrate that same budget in a smaller market, or a specific niche of the large market, you'll create a bigger impact and get noticed. That is why defining your niche (or specific market segment) is so important.

Your market niche is both defined by the segment you choose to target and based on the specific needs of the market you are trying to satisfy. What you specialize in, in terms of product and service features, also defines your niche market. Another way of putting it, you not only define your niche, your niche defines you.

This step focuses on helping you define your best market niche, but it is also vitally important that you optimize your products and services based on the wants, needs and desires of your market. Your product portfolio and attributes need to line up with the preferences of the market niche you target.

Another advantage of targeting a market niche is that it is usually more profitable. The more specialized your business (product or service), the greater your perceived value. Being known as a specialist or expert is a strong market position. The way to become recognized as an expert is to know more and more about less and less.

There is no question that marketing has evolved from a mass market to a niche market practice. Intuitive technology, self-customization, and on-demand offerings have literally brought us to a place where one-to-one marketing can be cost-effective.

Since most markets are now highly fragmented, the marketers who develop niche strategies, and offer tailored products and services, are the most successful. It is more important now than ever before to become proactive in defining and targeting your best market niche.

In fact, I suggest that you go beyond "defining" and "qualifying" your market, and go the extra step of "quantifying" its revenue potential. If you determine which market segment(s) to target prior to forecasting their sales potential, you could aim your resources at the wrong segment, especially if you aim merely at the "biggest market". Biggest isn't always best.

The rule of 80/20 is very much at play in virtually every market, meaning that a small percentage of a market generates a disproportionately large share of the business.

Tip: If you find that 20 percent of your market is generating 80 percent of your business, you should allocate your marketing resources accordingly, that is, 80 percent of your marketing budget, or more, should be trained on that 20 percent segment.

Niche Definition Exercise

Accurately defining and focusing on the best market niche involves a three-step process: 1) segment the market, 2) forecast sales potential, and 3) choose the target.

Step 1: Segment the Market

Segmenting is the process of subdividing a market universe of people who consume within a specific product category (such as automobile buyers) into smaller market segments, or affinity groups. These affinity groups are characterized and held together by having similar circumstances, values, and buying behaviors (such as SUV buyers). Another way of defining market segmentation is by the division of the market "pie" into segment "pieces."

Ford does not market their SUVs to everyone with a driver's license, only to those who fall into a defined market segment of

consumers who value the features and utility an SUV provides. To
effectively segment a market universe you need to know particular
information about its consumers.

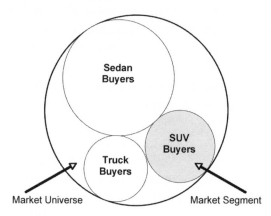

Consumer Markets

If your business sells to consumers (B2C), there are four criteria
you can use to segment your consumer market universe: *geographic*,
demographic, *psychographic*, and *behavior*.

☞ **Geographic** variables include region (from country to
zip code), population, density, climate, and topography.

☞ **Demographic** variables include gender, age, ethnic-
ity, religion, education, occupation, income, and family
unit.

☞ **Psychographic** variables include personality traits, life-
style, political persuasion, interests, activities, and beliefs.

☞ **Behavior** variables include benefits sought, usage rate,
brand loyalty, occasions of use, and readiness to buy.

All of the variables in these four segmentation criteria can be surfaced in the voice of your customer study (from Step 3). Thus, your in-depth interviews or focus groups can be extremely valuable for filling informational gaps. (Awareness of these variables in advance of your customer research preparation is a prime example of why I suggested earlier that you read this book entirely before doing all the exercises.)

You may have basic geographic and demographic data already in your customer database; if not, do your best to begin capturing it, i.e., age, gender, income, zip code, etc. The more information you possess on your existing customers, the more effective you will be at segmenting your market and targeting your offerings.

The voice of your customer can also inform you of their most prevalent psychographic and behavior affinities. These two criteria can be predictors of consumption through value questions on what customers care most and least about, and what they'd like to see changed, improved or added. If you are not tracking purchasing patterns, include questions in your VOC study to help determine what they buy, how much and how often. This information can be very useful to the process of segmenting your market and targeting a niche.

> Tip: Keep your segmenting process (data collection and analysis) as simple as possible. Don't create a headache for yourself; focus only on the information (variables) that are most relevant to your industry and marketing activities.

Business Markets

If your business sells to other businesses (B2B), the same segmenting process applies, but involves somewhat different criteria than what is used in segmenting consumer markets; they are: *geographic, corpographic, decision-maker* and *behavior.*

☞ **Geographic** variables include region (from country to zip code), headquarters, branch locations, and distribution.

☞ **Corpographic** variables include industry, size by revenue and employees, markets served, and years in business.

☞ **Decision-maker** variables include point-of-contact, influencers of buying decisions, and position titles.

☞ **Behavior** variables include benefits sought, usage rate, brand loyalty, and purchasing criteria and procedures.

Based on the segmentation variables most appropriate to your business, profile and document the characteristics that define each segment.

Step 2: Forecast Sales Potential

Forecasting the value (sales and revenue potential) of a market segment is easier to do for some industries than others. If your business is within a well-established industry, where there is a good deal of data from trade associations or other sources, forecasting could be simply a matter of crunching the numbers. But if yours is in a boutique or emerging industry, it will take more digging to uncover this information.

Forecasting segments provides important information that guides the targeting process. When forecasting market segments and trends, do your best in researching the available information, and make an educated guess. An "educated" guess (based on objective data) is far better than blindly picking a segment with no analysis.

You've probably heard the term WAG (wild-ass guess). Well, with some data informing your forecast, you can advance your WAG to SWAG (scientific wild-ass guess). (Hey, I don't make this stuff up, it's gospel to the trade.)

> "The only purpose of economic forecasting is to make astrology look respectable."
>
> *John Kenneth Galbraith,*
> *Economist and Best Selling Author*

Tip: If you have been in business for three or more years, review your own historical sales data. Otherwise, do research through Internet, trade associations, chambers of commerce, Small Business Administration, and other appropriate sources. Manufacturers and vendors can also be great sources of information because they have sales figures, and if you are a customer or prospect of theirs, they'll be motivated to help.

From whatever information is available for the industry, gather all you can of what's pertinent for quantifying the size and sales potential of your core market segments. Do your best to collect the size and sales information of each segment so you can estimate each segment's value on an annual revenue basis, and then compare. This information not only informs your targeting process, it will also be very useful when developing your sales forecast. You do sales forecasting...*right*?

Step 3: Choose the Target

Look at your market universe and, based on the rule of 80/20, target the core segment(s) with the greatest market potential. In determining the best segment, remember that bigger is not always better, especially if a segment is contracting or waning in size. Also bear in mind that some segments are more profitable than others. A good example is how Volvo (niche marketer) likely makes more profit per unit than Toyota (mass marketer) through targeting a small segment based on safety consciousness. With less competition to contend with in this niche, Volvo put itself into a strong position for capturing a greater market share of their target segment. Granted, Volvo sells less than 4 percent of what Toyota sells in terms of units, however, Volvo owns the "middle-class safety conscious" market segment.

Conventional wisdom suggests that the more consumers targeted, the more customers acquired. But remember the ink drop analogy. If you spread your marketing efforts too thin, sales will likely decline instead of grow. A more effective strategy is to focus on maintaining a "consistent market presence" in the most profitable segment(s).

Tip: Your marketing budget will determine how many segments you can target effectively. A tight budget dictates tight targeting.

Evaluate each segment using four targeting criteria: *response sensitivity*, *profitability*, *stability* and *accessibility*.

☞ **Response Sensitivity** is a determination of how responsive (willing and capable) a consumer is to purchase your product. When I was 18 years old I was quite "willing" to buy beer, but not legally "capable," so I was not "responsive" to Budweiser's selling proposition. A consumer who is highly motivated or interested in the benefits of your product or service would be characterized as response sensitive, if they have the capacity to buy.

☞ **Profitability** is another important segmenting criterion. Some consumers are more profitable to target than others because they purchase more product, or products with a higher profit margin. I have observed a phenomenon that I've labeled the "profit paradox." _The customers you spend the most amount of time with are likely the least profitable._ Most of us have experienced customers who are a "pain in the bum." My agency excluded...all of our clients are perfect! My point is that some customers, based on their purchasing behavior or service requirements, are less profitable than others. You want to target the most profitable niche.

☞ **Stability** of a market segment needs to be determined because you want to invest in building brand recognition and loyalty within a segment that is stable or expanding, not contracting. From a previous example, at the same time the personal computer market was expanding, sales for electronic typewriters were contracting. So, no matter how powerful your marketing program might be, you would hardly turn a profit selling typewriters in a digital era.

☞ **Accessibility** is also an important consideration as you determine which segment(s) to concentrate on. In other words, some consumer or business segments are easier to reach than others. If you cannot reach an appealing market segment, you should not waste your resources trying to attract that segment.

We had a client that was targeting CFOs in Fortune 500 companies. All of their attempts to connect with (and market to) these executives failed because they were very difficult to access. Based on our research, we determined that targeting the controller (a management level below the CFO) was more effective because they were far more accessible, and they pushed the product offer up to the CFO level for approval. Just by targeting a different "decision-maker" segment our client started to increase sales.

When targeting, you want to think about more than the segments themselves; you'll also need to consider your company's strengths and weakness, and those of your key competitors. Questions to ask are "What strengths do we have that are appealing to the various segments we can target?" and "What strengths do our competitors leverage, and who do they target?" Going after the same market segment (or niche) that your key competitors are targeting might not be the best strategy. So another question to ask might be, "Is there an underserved niche we can target or a gap in the competitive landscape we can fill?"

After you have gathered the information needed to segment your market universe, and forecasted each segment's revenue potential, compare the segments to define and prioritize the best niche(s) to target. The reason you go through this process? You guessed it: because *your opinion doesn't matter.*

Step 5 Exercise Summary:

After you have established your marketing budget, determine the best market niche to target by following this three-step process:

1   Divide your market universe into segments (affinity groups) having common situations and values based on industry appropriate variables (segmenting criteria).

2   With your historical and industry data, forecast the size and sales potential (profitability) of each segment.

3   Based on response sensitivity, profitability (sales potential), stability, and accessibility, prioritize the best market niche(s) to target.

Market Segmentation

Divide your market *universe* into *segments*, based on similar affinity characteristics and circumstances, for determining the best market niche(s) to target.

☞ **Segment the Market:**
Based on whether you sell to a consumer or business market, use the segmenting variables below to profile your primary market segments. The table below illustrates a B2C example.

Business Selling to Consumers (B2C)
- Geographic
- Demographic
- Psychographic
- Behavior

Business Selling to Businesses (2B)
- Geographic
- Corpographic
- Decision-maker
- Behavior

Variable	Segment A	Segment B	Segment C	R	P	S	A	Total
Geographic								
Demographic								
Psychographic								
Behavior								

Key: R = Response Sensitivity, P = Profitability, S = Stability, A = Accessibility

☞ **Forecast Sales Potential:**
Estimate the sales potential of your best segments, and determine which are the most profitable, by using your own sales records and available information from the sources below.
- Internet research
- Trade information
- Manufacturers
- Vendors

Calculation example: **Segment size   x   Avg Purchases per yr   =   Sales Potential**
                                  1,000 $500 $500,000

☞ **Choose the Target:**
After profiling your primary market segments, rank each on a score of 1 through 5 on the four targeting criteria (see Table Key above). Then total the scores to choose the best segment(s).

Ranking Key: 1 = Very Low, 2 = Low, 3 = Moderate, 4 = High, 5 = Very High

Shaping Your Position

"To get into the consumer's mind, you have to sacrifice.
You have to reduce the essence of your brand to a single
thought or attribute. An attribute that nobody else
already owns in your category."

Laura Ries
President, Ries & Ries, Bestselling Author

There are literally thousands of books on branding, and most are aimed at large business audiences. They are also more conceptual than concrete. That is because branding is not an exact science. If you ask 10 marketing experts for their definitions of branding, you'd likely get as many different answers. Not because any of them would be wrong, but because branding is a nebulous pseudoscience.

Unlike math, where one plus one always equals two, the process of branding is not a precise calculation. But the process does have some essential elements, and the MAP System breaks this process down to the prime building blocks of shaping an effective market position...one designed to grow your business.

Branding and Positioning

What is the difference between branding and positioning, and why do I focus predominantly on positioning?

"Brand is the 'f' word of marketing. People
swear by it, no one quite understands its
significance and everybody would like to
think they do it more often than they do"

Mark Di Soma,
Audacity Group

What is a brand? It identifies a company, product, service,
person, event or issue. It is whatever you want to be recognized
in your marketplace. The function of branding is to establish an
identity that sets your brand apart from other brands in your industry or category. Most people associate only a name and logo
with a brand, but these are merely two physical elements of a brand
(and the branding process).

From another perspective, a brand is created in the minds of
consumers based on their experience with it. Think about Starbucks. I believe their brand isn't about just coffee, it's also about
coffeehouses, communities and connections...it's about a social
experience. I see everything they do as in support of this perspective of the brand—from their product to their locations and retail
atmosphere. But mostly, their brand is about their people.

"It has always seemed to me that your
brand is formed primarily, not by what
your company says about itself,
but what the company does."

Jeff Bezos,
CEO, Amazon.com

Branding is what you do to be "known," whereas positioning is
what you do to be "known for something." Positioning is the value
you create and deliver based on what is important to your target
market. Your position also distinguishes your brand, in terms of

where you fit in your category, relative to competitors. It involves communicating a *unique* competency or attribute—known to be *valued* by the target market—as a means of competitively distinguishing a *proposition* from others in the same category. In other words, you *brand for identification*, you *position for differentiation*. And because brand identification requires effective differentiation, my focus is put largely on developing a meaningful and memorable market position for my clients.

What to Distinguish

So your question should be, "What should I distinguish in order to shape my position?" Here are a few thought starters using the 4-Ps of marketing: *product, price, place* and *promotion*.

Product

Many companies distinguish themselves on their product, service, and even packaging. Of the four, I believe a product (or service) distinction is the strongest, in terms of positioning.

With over 60 percent market share Heinz is the 800-pound gorilla in the catsup category. To remain in that position and sustain consumer loyalty, they developed a packaging innovation to further distinguish their brand.

I'm sure that Heinz (like most big brands) conducts market analyses similar to what I've outlined in this book. From my personal experience with the product packaging there were three primary frustrations: 1) it's hard to get the product out of the bottle, 2) can't get the last bit of catsup out of the bottle, and 3) when kids knock the glass bottle off the table it can break.

Heinz came up with the bottle we now all know and love, the upside-down, squeezable, plastic bottle. They even made the bottle thin enough to fit in a refrigerator door shelf. Eureka!

Here is another packaging example from a small business. A family friend of ours who owns a used car lot, O'Neill's Wheels, asked me for some marketing advice. His lot is situated on "auto row" with several competitors all on the same drag in very close proximity.

When I went out to meet with him, I noticed that all of the car lots, including his, looked identical. They all had the same red, white and blue bunting, ribbons and flags.

In a bold move the Irish owner took my advice to change the colors of everything on his lot to Irish green, including a very big building. He even switched all of the red, white and blue streamers to green. His lot now stands out among all of the other lots. I mean, it looks like a beacon shining through the fog. Five years later, his "new customer exit interviews" still reveal the color of the lot as the number one reason customers stopped by. It grabbed their attention. People in the community still talk about the Irish guy with the green car lot. Wouldn't you like your community talking about you?

Price

In general, small businesses don't overprice their products and services, they under price. They think they need to have a low price to compete.

The most frequent complaint I hear (especially from retailers) is, "I can't compete with the big box stores on price or stock." It's true, they can't. This is why *price* is my least favorite positioning strategy, except for premium brands. Keep in mind, however, price is what you pay, value is what you receive. There are many other ways to deliver value than by lowering price. Coffee is a commodity, yet Starbucks doesn't position its brand on price, in fact, their coffee is among the most expensive. The value they offer includes a comfortable atmosphere where you can hang out to meet friends and business associates, and have a good latte prepared by really friendly people.

You don't need to be a big brand in order to take a page out of the big brands' playbook and apply it to your small business. In the Seattle area, McLendon Hardware is a family owned business with multiple locations and 400 employees. They continue to grow in spite of going head to head with two Fortune 500 companies, Home Depot and Lowe's. Even during a down economy, McLendon Hardware never loses sight of growing its business.

They do it by delivering on their brand promise, "Where People Make the Difference." While that tagline is by no means unique, the customer experience they consistently deliver is competitively superior. They pride themselves on hiring people who have experience in the field, with unbeatable product knowledge. And they go the extra mile on service by walking their customers to the product and listening to understand their projects so they can give advice. They continue to thrive because of their people, not their prices.

Place

Place refers to location, delivery and distribution. Some companies use a distribution strategy to distinguish their brands, most recently in online and mobile e-commerce. After online banking became the norm, Bank of America was one of the first to distinguish itself by launching its mobile banking service…so customers could do banking over their cell phones.

Dell changed the way consumers shop for computers, online instead of at a retail outlet. Dell computers are completely customizable and delivered to your front door. Similarly, some locally owned grocery outlets offer home delivery, a service highly valued by a burgeoning senior market segment.

One of my favorite distribution quotes goes back to 1923, when Coca Cola CEO Robert Woodruff said, "Put Coke within arm's reach of desire." In a small agency's effort to place their service "within arm's reach of desire," WorkSource Snohomish County expanded their market coverage by developing a strategic alliance with the County's library system. Before the alliance they didn't have the resources to expand beyond three offices, but today they have 14 additional locations serving their County of 2,090 square miles. Again, you don't have to be big to be innovative.

Promotion

In many product categories there is very little difference among competitors. This is especially true in categories that are perceived as commodities (sometimes called parity categories), where price is the primary difference between seemingly identical products or services. This is when promotional tactics can separate players in a market space cluttered with clones. Some examples:

United Parcel Service (UPS): "What can 'Brown' do for you?" In 2002 they launched the most aggressive ad campaign in their 95-year history. Its only recognizable distinction was the color brown. Did it work? No, if you measure their financial performance against their biggest competitor. When they launched the campaign, their revenue share ratio was 1.56 above FedEx. In 2010, eight years later, that ratio had dropped to 1.28. They lost ground...by nearly 18 percent.

GEICO: (what a *green Gecko lizard* can do). In 2000, the GEICO Gecko was introduced. Before then, not many people knew about GEICO other than Warren Buffet (who has been a shareholder since 1951). By 2010, GEICO was considered the fastest growing personal auto insurance company in the U.S., while State Farm, the category leader in 2000, had dropped from 15th to 34th on the Fortune 500 list (2000-2010),

So why did the "Gecko" outperform "Brown"? The answer is that GEICO has a single message being consistently driven home, *"15 minutes can save you 15% or more on your car insurance."* What single message comes to mind from UPS's advertising? If you are scratching your head, you're not alone.

Al Ries and Laura Ries, co-authors of *The 22 Immutable Laws of Branding*, refer to this as the "Law of Singularity" which suggests that you consistently communicate a single idea, attribute or concept. Of course, GEICO's $800 million dollar annual advertising budget may have something to do with their success, too.

Unique Value Proposition

Now that you have some ideas of what other companies have done to distinguish themselves, let's explore how you can go about doing the same: by shaping your position.

You start by determining your Unique Value Proposition (UVP), which is the foundation of an effective market position.

There are three non-negotiable components in a unique value proposition:

☞ It must distinguish your brand as competitively unique;

☞ The distinction must be valued by your target market;

☞ You must position your brand as being the *first*, *best* or *only* in your product category, and within your geographic footprint.

UVP Exercise

Developing your UVP involves a three-step process: 1) select core competencies, 2) determine competitor vulnerabilities, and 3) identify customer values.

Step 1: Select Core Competencies

Your core competenes are qualities or features (within your marketing mix) that really stand out as significant strengths. Hopefully, these strengths surfaced during your SWOT Analysis (from Step 2). If not, the analysis exposed a competency gap that needs to be addressed before you can develop an effective unique value proposition.

In that case, you would go back and review your voice of your customer data for values and preferences that you could leverage from a positioning perspective, and then focus on adding or enhancing features that best align with your customers' wants, needs and desires.

Step 2: Determine Competitor Vulnerabilities

After you've listed your core competencies, review the information collected from the secret shops (Step 4) you conducted on your key competitors. Compare your core competencies to the strengths and weaknesses of your competitors. The purpose of this comparison is to determine which among your core competencies line up against your competitors' vulnerabilities, weaknesses or gaps in the competitive landscape.

> "Concentrate your strengths against your competitor's relative weaknesses."
>
> *Bruce Henderson,*
> *CEO, Boston Consulting Group*

You are looking for anything you do (or something about your offer) that is unique or better than what your key competitors do or offer. This will reduce your *core competencies* list down to a shorter list of *competitively unique competencies.*

If none of your core competencies show up as being competitively unique or superior, you'll need to address that gap as well. In that case, compare your customer values (from your VOC data) to your competitors' weaknesses and look for a customer desire that is not being satisfied by your competitors, one that you can fulfill.

Step 3: Identify Customer Values

The last step involves comparing your unique competencies with your customer values. Review the VOC data from your in-depth interviews or focus groups (Step 3). Create a list of what your customers said they value most, and their most important decision factors when choosing between brands.

Your goal in this final step is to identify the single thing you do, better or different than your key competitors, which aligns best with what your customers value most.

This single quality, feature or attribute will be the foundation of your UVP, and will shape your market position. Your UVP will take the form of a short sentence that communicates what is unique about your offering (relative to competitors' weaknesses), what is of value (that customers care most about), and your proposition (that is first, best or only). Once you are clear on what your UVP is, it should drive all of your marketing and growth strategy decisions.

Create Tagline and Key Messages

From your UVP, develop a catchy tagline that you'll use in all of your promotion to communicate why your target audience should choose your brand over others. Then craft key messages in support of your tagline to give more clarity to your market position, so your audience really understands how they will benefit greater as your customer or client.

After you have come up with a few potential taglines based on your UVP, that are short (three to five words) and catchy (memorable and meaningful), run them past some of your best customers, because *it's your customer's opinion that counts*. Let them chose their favorite taglines, and allow suggestions. As importantly, ask them "why" they chose what they did.

(Recall that in Step 3 [Asking Your Customers] we addressed how the "why" is as important as the "what.")

Tip: Your customers' response to "why" they like a particular tagline will guide you in creating key messages. When asking "why" probe for the emotion behind the rational answer.

Producing a tagline and key messages involves a creative process. If you have the budget, contracting with a professional will likely produce the best results.

Positioning Example

I can confidently say that, like nearly all big brands, GEICO does customer and competitor research, and from the position they created, I surmise that these two things surfaced: 1) their customers' purchasing behavior is driven primarily by price, and 2) there is a reluctance to switch carriers because the process is perceived as being a hassle or taking too long.

GEICO likely used that information to position itself. First they distinguished their brand using a cute little Gecko with an adorable accent. Then they positioned their brand with the tagline *"15 minutes can save you 15% or more on your car insurance."* A long tagline, granted, but it directly addresses the primary desire and concern of its industry's consumers. Since Berkshire Hathaway bought GEICO in 1996, GEICO's market share has grown by 324 percent (and the Gecko is still in play).

Subcategory

It can be difficult to come up with a competitively unique competency that will be valued by your customers and will position your brand as being the first, best or only in your product category. This challenge is especially true if you are in a competitively cluttered category. If you can't distinguish your brand in your category, an effective positioning technique is to create a subcategory that you can own.

Our agency came to this very crossroad with a client in the banking category. A small community bank, they were competing with national brands. We were not able to distinguish our client in the banking category, but we were successful in creating a subcategory where the bank could be the best. We positioned them as the "#1 Local SBA Lender" which they were in the County they served. People (in both consumer and business markets) want to work with "#1". We had to add the word "local" to the tagline because there was a national bank that had more SBA loans than our client.

Because this local community bank executed their promotion so well, by communicating the same message to the same market niche consistently over time, two things happened: 1) their SBA loan portfolio grew significantly, and 2) after a couple of years, they exceeded the national bank in SBA loans within their County.

Whether you position yourself in your category or create a subcategory, if you competitively distinguish your brand based on customer values, you can accelerate the growth of your business. We've used this exact system for hundreds of small businesses, and it works remarkably well when you implement it correctly by aligning your promotion and optimizing your results: the next two steps.

Step 6 Exercise Summary:

After you have collected and organized your SWOT, VOC and competitor information, Develop your UVP by following this three-step process:

1   Create a list of all your core competencies (major strengths) by reviewing your SWOT asset priorities.

2   Determine which of your core competencies are unique by comparing them against your competitors' relative weaknesses and gaps.

3   Evaluate your competitively unique competencies alongside your customer values to identify the most important attribute to establish your UVP and tagline.

Unique Value Proposition

Developing a unique value proposition is the process of distinguishing your brand from competitors in a way that is valued by your target market.

☞ **Select Core Competencies:**
Review the results of your SWOT analysis, specifically your strengths list, and select a list of core competencies that may distinguish your brand from your key competitors. List your core competencies:

_____

_____

☞ **Determine Competitor Vulnerabilities:**
Review the secret shop results of your key competitors and compare your core competencies to their relative weaknesses. Determine which of your core competencies are unique or superior. List your unique competencies:

_____

_____

☞ **Identify Customer Values:**
Review the voice of your customer data, specifically responses related to what your customers most value, as well as their most important deciding factors when choosing between brands. List customer values:

_____

_____

Use the information above to populate a competitor comparison table. Based on your strengths and competitor shops choose the most appropriate characteristics to compare. Example below.

Characteristics	Your Company	Competitor 1	Competitor 2	Competitor 3
Target Market				
Product Focus				
Special Features				
Market Position				
Customer Service				
Guarantee				

Aligning Your Promotion

"How well we communicate is determined not by how well we say things, but by how well we are understood."

Andrew Grove,
Former President, CEO and Chairman, Intel

To be successful in promoting your company, product or service (your brand), "you only need to do four things right":

☞ Deliver the right message;
☞ To the right market;
☞ Through the right channel;
☞ At the right time.

Obviously, doing these four things "right" is easier said than done! This tale illustrates the point.

A Minneapolis couple decided to go to Florida during a particularly icy winter. They planned on staying at the same hotel where they spent their honeymoon 20 years earlier.

Because of hectic schedules, it was difficult to coordinate their travel. So, the husband flew to Florida on Thursday, with his wife to fly down the following day.

The husband checked into the hotel. There was a computer in his room, so he decided to send an email to his wife. However, he accidentally left out one letter in her email address, and without realizing his error, sent the email.

Meanwhile, somewhere in Houston, a widow had just returned home from her husband's funeral. He was a minister who had passed away following a heart attack.

The widow decided to check her email expecting messages from relatives and friends. After reading the first message, she screamed and fainted. The widow's son rushed into the room, found his mother on the floor, and saw the computer screen which read:

> To: My Loving Wife
> Subject: I've Arrived
>
> I know you're surprised to hear from me. They have computers here now and you are allowed to send emails to your loved ones. I've just arrived and have been checked in. I've seen that everything has been prepared for your arrival tomorrow.
>
> Looking forward to seeing you then!!!! Hope your journey is as uneventful as mine was.
>
> P.S. Sure is freaking hot down here!!!!

This was the right message sent through the right channel at the right time, but to the wrong market. The brutal reality is that in order to generate the best return on investment, even three out of four won't cut it. But by following the MAP System you can do all four things "right".

We tackled *market* in Step 5 (Defining Your Niche), hence targeting the right market. Step 6 demonstrated how to shape your position, which is the guidance system for developing a *message* that resonates with your target market. Because that is so essential to growing your business, we'll delve a little deeper into how to develop the "right message" later in this step.

First, we'll address the third and fourth things you need to "do right," *channel* and *timing*, beginning with the types of promotion to get you thinking about your channel options.

Promotion

There are many ways to promote your brand and offer. Most fall into one of four primary categories: *advertising, publicity, sales promotion,* and *personal selling.* This is not intended as an in-depth itemization of how to tactically promote your brand; rather, an overview that highlights your channel options.

Advertising

Traditional advertising includes any paid form of communications, e.g., television, radio, print (newspapers and magazines), and out-of-home media (billboards, bus boards, and any other advertising that is experienced outside of the home).

Direct marketing and e-marketing are also forms of advertising. Direct marketing, because it targets individuals, is more selective than advertising to a mass market. The most common types of direct marketing are direct mail and telemarketing, and they are usually associated with a specific offer or incentive to purchase.

E-marketing includes all forms of online communications, such as website and email marketing. E-marketing tactics also include Search Engine Optimization (SEO) and Search Engine Marketing (SEM). The purpose of SEO is to improve your position on search engine indexes, such as Google, Bing and Yahoo. The purpose of SEM is to drive traffic to your site through paid key words, e.g., through Google AdWords. This form of advertising has become increasingly popular because it can be relatively inexpensive (controllable), very targetable, and easy to measure.

Another popular form of advertising is sponsorship of an event, team or organization. Some marketing professionals categorize sponsorship with publicity. I categorize it as advertising because there is a cost. Trade shows, exhibits and fairs also fall into the advertising category for the same reason.

Publicity

While advertising refers to paid media, publicity refers to earned media. I call it "earned" instead of "free" because publicity is not free—it costs time and talent to do it right. The most commonly recognized form of publicity is public relations (PR), also referred to as media relations. To be successful in PR, establishing relationships with the appropriate media outlet staff is important. That, and your story must be newsworthy and suitably targeted. Other forms of publicity include events, such as press events, an open house, and grand openings. Most events are supported with advertising.

I also classify social media, online networking, and blogging as forms of publicity because typically the only cost is time and talent. To say that social media is a burgeoning type of promotion would be an understatement. Marketers are learning how to integrate social media and blogging tactics with their other forms of promotion; however, social media should not be used for sales promotion per se. As a business tool it is designed to stimulate conversations between marketers and consumers. If you try to overtly sell through social media, that tactic may backfire.

Sales Promotion

This type of promotion is designed to "pull" consumers in the door and "push" product out the door. Popular forms, especially in retail, include point-of-sale displays such as end-caps (end of aisle displays), shelf-talkers, bottle-neckers, and point-of-sale signage. Sales promotion tactics include, but are not limited to, price incentives, coupons, samples, rebates, gifts with purchase, and some forms of loyalty programs.

Personal Selling

Selling involves a person or sales force actively selling products or services to individuals with the intent of converting prospects into customers. Personal selling is often conducted in tandem with other types of promotion. Selling is a person-to-person (but not always face-to-face) promotion tactic common in retail and business-to-business sectors, and designed to "close a sale."

Your promotional mix (combination of promotional channels) should be based on your marketing objectives, target market, budget, and competitors' promotions.

Tip: Select your channels for promotion before developing your key messages. The channel(s) you select will determine your copy density. For example: A billboard would only have a few words communicating a single key point; a print ad can be much more detailed in copy.

Channel Selection

There are a multitude of options when it comes to selecting channels (modes of communication) for delivering your message. The most common mistake I see small businesses make is basing their buying decision on price. My first question to a new client is, "Why did you choose that channel?" The response I most often hear is, "I got a great deal." I follow with, "How's that working out for you?" That's when I usually get a blank stare. Who cares how cheap the channel is if it doesn't work?

I was in advertising sales in the '80s, and no offense to my ad sales brethren, but their job is to sell their inventory. Just because an ad rep offers you a "great deal" doesn't mean it's in your best interest to buy.

You'd likely pay a million dollars a month in advertising gladly if it generated two million in return. And I bet you wouldn't pay $50 a month if you only received $25 in return. Your key considerations should be *budget*, *efficiency*, and *VOC data*. Not price.

Budget

Before evaluating your options, set your promotion budget. The amount you have available to spend will determine which and how many communications channels are most appropriate. For a small budget, you'll likely need to concentrate on the single most cost effective channel, rather than a mix of channels if you have a larger budget.

It is best to set up and allocate your budget based on the timing of your promotion (covered later in this step).

A question I often hear is, "How much should I spend on advertising (promotion)?" Or, "What percentage of sales should I be spending?" The answer is normally somewhere in the range of 1 to 15 percent of sales. That is a wide range, and where your specific budget falls within or outside that range will be based on standards in your industry, the level of competition in your space, your level of brand recognition, and how aggressive you want to be.

If you have strong brand recognition with little competition, your budget could be relatively low. If you are in a very competitive market, with relatively low brand recognition, your budget should be as aggressive as possible.

Using either present or forecasted sales, here are two ways of calculating your promotion budget as a percentage of sales:

☞ Base your percentage on gross revenue if you have low COGS (Cost Of Goods Sold), e.g., a high margin service business.

☞ Base your percentage on gross profit (gross revenue minus COGS) if you have high COGS, e.g., a manufacturer requiring raw materials.

Efficiency

Remember the dilution principle covered in Step 5 (Defining Your Niche)? This is where it meets *reach* and *frequency*. Spreading your promotion budget incorrectly between the two will not produce an efficient buy or positive return on your investment.

Your determination of which channels to select will be objectively based on which ones are reaching the right market as *frequently* as possible within your budget, resulting in the best cost *efficiency*.

☞ **Reach** refers to how broadly you can deliver your message; how widely you can extend your reach to a greater percentage of your target market depends on the size of your budget.

☞ **Frequency** refers to the number of times each person you reach experiences your message, and it is most often the more important of the two measures, especially for smaller budgets.

To get your audience's attention, and instill recall of your brand and offering, their frequent exposure to your message is paramount. That's why increased frequency is usually a better bet than extended reach. In other words, reaching a smaller audience more frequently will generate more sales than targeting a larger audience less frequently. This is the case because, as a society, we are way oversaturated with promotional messages.

Being effective in promotion also requires that you communicate the same message to the same audience consistently over time. I often remind my clients that, just about the time they start getting sick and tired of their promotion, that's the time it will start working in the marketplace.

☞ **Efficiency** is what you get if you properly balance reach and frequency. You will make your channel selections based on each channel's efficiency in reaching your target market, as frequently as possible, for the budget available. That is a far better measuring stick than price. When working with ad sales reps, the key is to make apples-to-apples comparisons by using the same time period and budget. Ask them for the cost-per-thousand (CPM) of

the schedule being proposed, and require these four criteria: 1) include only your target audience, not the total
audience reached by the channel, 2) base the CPM on
gross impressions (reach multiplied by frequency), 3) include only the promotion schedule period, and 4) include
the total cost of production.

Channel	Ad Budget	Gross Imp	Production	CPM
WABC	$10,000	250,000	$5,000	$60
The Post	$10,000	200,000	$0	$50

In the example above the ad budget is the same (as it should be
when comparing channels). WABC delivers 25 percent more gross
impressions for the budget, however, when the production charge is
factored into the calculation, the CPM is 20 percent higher (or less
efficient). Your goal is to negotiate the lowest CPM as possible.

It is important to note that no media measuring system fully accounts for the production values of the various media. A TV spot
may have more appeal because it consists of audio, visual and mo-
tion, but that production value comes at a cost. A radio spot only has
audio, but can be produced at no cost, so there are trade-offs. A print
ad allows far more copy detail than a bus board but that doesn't mean
print is better than a bus board. TV is more dynamic than print but
that doesn't mean TV is better than print. Each format has its advan-
tages and disadvantages. You'll need to weigh your options based on
your objectives, target market, and budget.

Tip: Different channel formats use different efficiency measures, e.g., broadcast uses cost-per-
point (CPP) instead of cost-per-thousand (CPM);
but, if you incorporate the four efficiency criteria
stated earlier, CPM can be used as an apples-to-
apples comparison across all channel formats.

VOC Data

If you actively promote your brand, asking your customers about their channel usage is important. Based on your channel selection, query your customers about their choices in that channel. For example, if you decide the channel of radio provides the most efficient coverage, then ask your customers for their favorite radio station. This information will guide your selection process.

If your budget allows, you may want to consult an objective expert to help you land on the optimal selection of channels. Even if you cannot afford expert consultation, your ad rep wants you to succeed and will provide you with useful research. Just keep in mind that an ad rep's job is to sell you the channel's inventory. If you consult several ad reps and make CPM comparisons, you'll be able to make an informed selection.

Timing Your Promotion

The last (and easiest) of the four things you need to "do right" is to align the timing of your promotion to coincide with the purchasing patterns of your target market. For example, Hallmark knows that the bulk of their sales will occur based on holidays, so for Valentine's Day their timing is obvious.

But if your sales are spread out fairly evenly throughout the year, timing will require more thinking. In that case, the things to consider are *sales cycles*, *scheduling*, and *competitor promotion*.

Sales Cycles

Even if your sales are spread out, most likely there are sales periods of peaks and valleys (busier and slower times). For busy periods (peaks) you *follow the season*, for slower periods (valleys) you *fill in the gaps*.

☞ **Follow the season** is the "make hay while the sun shines" approach. You allocate your promotional budget to hit the street just before the market peaks, so you can be top-of-mind when consumers start to think about purchasing in your product category. This involves both micro and macro cycles. A weekend is an example of a micro cycle. There are more new cars purchased on weekends, consequently you see more car dealer advertising at the end of almost every week. A period lasting for a season is an example of a macro cycle. In early spring, homeowners begin thinking about products in the lawn and garden category.

☞ **Fill in the gaps** is the opposite of the "follow the season" approach. You schedule your promotion for slower sales periods, typically in micro cycles. Think about the last time you saw or used a coupon for a popular restaurant. The offer was most likely limited to certain days and times, such as Sunday through Thursday from 4:00 p.m. to 6:00 p.m., but not Friday and Saturday evenings, particularly between 6:00 p.m. and 8:00 p.m., when popular restaurants are at capacity.

Based on your sales cycles and capacity, consider which approach, *follow the season* or *fill in the gaps*, would generate the greatest return on investment.

Scheduling

There are four standard methods of scheduling promotion: *continuity, concentration, flighting* and *pulsing*.

☞ **Continuity** means spreading your promotional budget evenly throughout the year, that is, you are promoting nonstop. GEICO, for example, is constantly advertising through a mix of channels. Because this is a very costly method, it is not used by many small businesses.

☞ **Concentration** involves allocating an entire promotion budget to one or a few promotional periods, most often associated with a sales promotion. Nordstrom, a high-end department store, concentrates on their Half Yearly Sale, but they do not do much advertising otherwise.

☞ **Flighting** is the choice of most small businesses because it stretches the budget while creating the illusion of non-stop advertising. You advertise on and off throughout the year (two weeks on, two weeks off, or one week every month, for example). Wal-Mart appears to use "flighting" to promote their brand and product offerings. They are not constantly advertising like GEICO, but they seem to be. For flighting to be effective, consistency in schedule is important.

We run ads in every issue of a monthly business journal for a client of ours on a limited budget, who is in the office technology category. This is a smart flighting consistency for them because a monthly business journal has a much longer shelf life than the business section of a daily newspaper, and far less expensive than advertising every week. And because they are in every monthly issue they have a consistent presence.

☞ **Pulsing** is an approach used mostly by big brands. It combines the methods of *continuity* (at a lower spending level) and *flighting* (to deliver a stronger burst, usually timed seasonally or to a sales promotion). Budweiser advertises fairly consistently throughout the year, but less frequently than GEICO. And there are certain times of the year when Budweiser really ratchets up their spending level, in addition to their continuity schedule, for major sporting events, such as the NFL Super Bowl and Olympics.

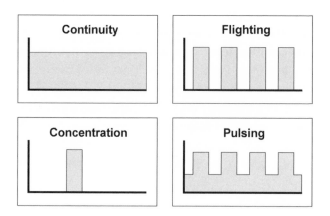

Key: Vertical axis = Dollars, Horizontal axis = Time

Competitor Promotion

The promotion timing of your key competitors also needs to be factored into your timing decision. Based on your competitor study from Step 4, you will know what and when your key competitors are promoting. You might choose to align your promotion timing with the competition (because of your industry's sales cycles), or at different times (to stand out in the crowd).

Sometimes purposely advertising at different times than your competitors can pay off. If I were in a retail product category, where all of my competitors were advertising a Memorial Day Sale, I'd advertise ahead of them, promoting a Pre-Memorial Day Sale, to get a jump on the competition. Just as you want your market position to stand out, you want the same for your promotion.

In consideration of your promotion budget, choose the timing and scheduling based on your sales cycles, capacity and competitor promotion.

Key Messages Exercise

After you have selected the best promotion channels and timing, you'll be ready to begin crafting messages that support your tagline (based on your unique value proposition), and that grab the attention of your audience. This will require creativity, and it is important that your creativity be guided by research-based strategy.

> "Creative without strategy is called art.
> Creative with strategy is called advertising."
>
> *Jef I. Richards*
> *Advertising Department Chairman*
> *University of Texas*

Developing key messages and effective promotional copy involves a three-step process: 1) define communications objective, 2) set the hook, and 3) create simple messages.

Step 1: Define Communications Objective

Before developing your audience and channel-appropriate messages (copy), it is important to be clear on what your communications objective is. What are you attempting to accomplish, what action or presence are you trying to generate in your market?

If you are trying to get your audience to take action, then your message will be different than if you merely wanted to generate brand awareness. Because most small businesses don't have huge promotion budgets, it's even more critical for their dollars to deliver a return on investment. That's why I usually recommend incorporating a "call-to-action" in the copy.

Tip: This is another way your ad rep can help. Ad reps know their media and how to use them most effectively. If you don't have experience writing promotional copy, ask your rep for guidance. Remember, they want you to be successful so they can keep you as a client. Most reps provide great service.

Step 2: Set the Hook

In all cases of promotion, your message needs to cut through the clutter. Depending on which report you read, the average person is bombarded with between 1,500 and 3,000 brand messages every day. Your target audience is oversaturated.

The most effective way of cutting through the clutter is to use a *hook* to grab your audience's attention. Your hook can take the form of a compelling headline, graphic or photo, anything that will stop your audience in their tracks and cause them to take notice. The only purpose of a hook is to grab your audience's attention, nothing more, nothing less. So don't get too clever or verbose. You can find ideas for headlines and hooks that resonate with your target audience by reviewing the voice of your customer data.

Step 3: Create Simple Messages

After you have an attention-getting hook, you'll add some detail that elevates your audience from awareness to interest (even desire). The best way to keep from losing your audience (after getting their attention) is to keep your message simple, concise, and focused on benefits.

Most messages are either too complex or drawn out. Your message might seem clear to you, but remember, good communication is determined by how well you are understood. Since you eat, sleep and breathe your brand, it's easy for you to assume that what is clear to you will be understood by your audience also. Be sure and test your messages for concept clarity before using them. Generally, in copy-writing, less is more and simple is better.

In addition to crafting your messages with clarity, you need to address potential barriers that may keep your audience from taking action. This is particularly important if you don't have strong brand recognition. Your audience will likely have three top-of-mind questions that your message should answer:

- ☞ What's In It For Me (WIIFM)?
- ☞ Why should I trust you?
- ☞ Why should I buy now?

Emotion vs. Logic

Keep in mind that the primary purpose of most promotion (specifically advertising) is to make an emotional connection with the target audience. For that reason you don't want your messages to include everything and the kitchen sink. Rather, limit what they say to the relevant and emotionally compelling.

Consumers often justify their purchases (after the fact) with logic, but it was an emotion that closed the deal. This phenomenon is called *post-hoc rationalization*. The human brain works this way, making decisions based on unconscious emotions, without our conscious awareness.

Neale Martin, Ph.D., in his book *Habit*, explains that we grossly underestimate how much behavior is under the sway of our unconscious mind, that it controls 95 percent of our behavior. Here's a personal example that illustrates Dr. Martin's theory.

When I bought my last car, it was purely an emotional decision. It was a completely loaded, sporty red Acura TL... fastest car I've ever owned. Nothing could be more emotional to a red-blooded male, but rationalizing the purchase to my wife, I attempted to use logic, of course.

On my way home from the dealership, I called my wife on the hands free blue tooth phone to share the exciting news. "Oh honey," I said, "I just bought a brand new car. It's a pretty red Acura. It gets

30 mpg on the freeway." Continuing to justify my tail off, I go on, "And you'll love the navigation system. You'll never get lost again! Come outside, I'm pulling in the drive way right now."

As I set the parking break, I noticed Sandra was already standing in the doorway. I waved enthusiastically, and then made the mistake of racing the engine. Busted! She gave me "the look," the kind of look a husband deserves after 20 years of bliss. She rolled her eyes, turned around and walked back inside.

So much for logic! I'm sure by now it's clear that my issues go far beyond being potty trained at gunpoint.

Step 7 Exercise Summary:

After you've determined who to target and what market position will resonate best, develop effective key messages by following this three-step process:

1   Determine your promotion objectives and budget.
2   Develop an attention-getting hook to cut through the clutter and cause your target audience to take notice.
3   Based on the channel(s) you select, create simple key messages (copy) that elevates your audience from awareness to interest by addressing values and concerns.

Key Messages

After you have selected the best promotion channels begin crafting messages, that support your Unique Value Proposition (UVP) and tagline, to grab your audience's attention.

☞ **Define Communications Objective:**
It is important to be clear on what your communications objective is, and what you are attempting to accomplish, in terms of the action or presence that you want to generate.

Write your communications objective:

_____

_____

☞ **Set the Hook:**
To grab your audience's attention, your hook should be a compelling headline, graphic or photo—anything that will stop your audience in their tracks and cause them to take notice.

Based on your VOC data write hook ideas:

_____

_____

☞ **Create Simple Messages:**
To keep from losing your audience it is important to keep your message simple, concise, and focused on benefits. Begin by addressing the three questions that most customers have:

What's in it for me (WIIFM)?

_____

Why should I trust you?

_____

Why should I buy now?

_____

Based on your UVP, your VOC data, and answers to the three questions above, craft three to five simple and concise key messages, and test them with a few customers.

Optimizing Your Results

"If you don't pre-test and post-track your marketing stimulus, you'll never know how to fully optimize your results."

Andrew Ballard,
President, Marketing Solutions, Inc.

You're on the home stretch. Based on your market analysis, you have developed sound positioning and promotion strategies to grow your business. Now it's time to implement, but you still have a few to-dos before you go-to-market.

Because MAPS is research-based, your growth strategies should generate appreciable results, but that's not to say your results will be optimal. There is always room for improvement.

Optimizing your results requires that, before launching your promotion, you pre-test everything that your customers and prospective customers may experience. It also requires that you post-track everything you have launched so you can make informed adjustments to improve your return on investment.

Pre-Test Exercise

We always share our "test before you invest" mantra with our clients. Pre-testing will not only optimize your results, it will save you money too. We pre-test promotion especially if it is integrated with a campaign (advertising, publicity and sales promotion).

The purpose of pre-testing is to make sure your promotion will meet your objectives and create the desired results. It involves a three-step process: 1) develop the concept, 2) recruit test group, and 3) optimize your promotion.

Step 1: Develop the Concept

After you have selected your promotion channels and developed your key messages (hook and copy), produce a mockup (or dummy ad) to present to your test group. You may need to work with a professional to create a mockup. The purpose is to not spend much, if any, money on production before you get customer feedback. Often the media that you buy will provide no-cost or low-cost mockups for your promotion.

Concepts for such media as print, website, out-of-home, and most sales promotion materials are simple to mockup and present because they can be printed from a computer. Audio and visual media are a bit more complex, but you can still get your concept across to a test group without going to the expense of a "full production."

If you selected radio as a promotion channel, the station you are buying will produce what is called a "spec spot" to play for your test group at no cost. If you plan on using TV, you have two options: 1) create a storyboard in print or PowerPoint, or 2) do a low budget video production.

The key point is that you want to give your test group a clear understanding of the promotion, using messages and images to simulate the actual promotion, so they can provide meaningful feedback.

Step 2: Recruit Test Group

You don't need a big budget to assemble a test group (also referred to as a focus group or consumer jury) for acquiring feedback on your promotion.

Tip: It is always best to recruit your test group from people who are consumers of what you sell.

You can present a mockup of concepts, images, headlines and key copy points to a test group for ascertaining what kind of reception you'll get from your promotion. You can also use a test group for brainstorming ideas and prioritizing product features. We have used focus groups for feedback during development of websites, sale promotion materials, and new product names. They have reviewed and critiqued advertisement elements for us, even evaluated press releases prior to distribution.

A very inexpensive way to conduct a test group is by developing a *customer advisory council* from your existing customer base. We've had great success recruiting these councils for our clients because test groups are fun, and customers usually feel honored to be asked for their opinions because they know *it's your customer's opinion that counts.*

For one of our health care clients we recruited 15 patients to serve a one-year term and meet quarterly for a 90-minute lunch. This is not a huge commitment. Participants enjoy free lunches and a chance to network among people who have something in common with each other.

Each quarter they are presented with many different mockups, from website and brochures to radio spec spots and newspaper ads. They choose headlines, prioritize features, and brainstorm promotional ideas...and they absolutely love it. Typically we get between 10 and 12 people to show up, and it only costs our client 12 box lunches. We even conduct these group meetings in the hospital so there is no facility cost.

Tip: Recruit a new group of customers every year to serve on your council to keep from burning anyone out, and to ensure a continuously fresh perspective. Also be sure that your council represents your best customers, the ones you want to duplicate.

I can't count how many times it has been pointed out in a test group that a mockup (message) is confusing. Most messages are made too complex, as I mentioned earlier (in Step 7). Marketers often wrongly assume the target audience will understand their message, or they omit minor details they assume will be understood.

My favorite illustration of this point is a story called, "Sometimes it does take a rocket scientist."

Scientists at NASA needed to simulate collisions with airborne fowl to test the strength of windshields. So they built a cannon specifically to launch dead chickens at the windshields of their space shuttles.

British engineers heard about it and were eager to test the windshields on their new high-speed trains. Arrangements were made and the cannon was shipped. When the cannon was first fired, the British engineers stood in shock as they watched the chicken shoot out of the barrel, crash through the shatter-proof windshield, smash the control console to bits, break the engineer's backrest in two, and embed itself in the back of the cabin like an arrow shot from a bow.

Horrified, they sent NASA the disastrous results and specifications of their experiment. They begged the U.S. scientists for suggestions. NASA responded with a one-line memo: "Thaw the Chicken."

Sometimes truth is stranger than fiction. Anyway you get the point. Don't assume your messages are clearly understood by your audience, no matter how smart you think they are. By using a test group, you can "thaw the chicken" before you go-to-market.

Step 3: Optimize Your Promotion

After running your promotion concepts, hooks, images and copy past your customer advisory council, optimize your promotion by making the appropriate changes based on their feedback. Often a small change can make a big difference.

Another method of optimizing promotion, without using a test group, is an A/B Test. Most often used by direct marketers and Internet advertisers, an A/B test is conducted by distributing concept

A (the control concept) to half the audience, and concept B (the test concept) to the other half. Then the results are tracked. Decades ago, this technique was pioneered by direct mail experts. They would split their mailing list in half and send out two different versions of the same piece to determine the optimal combination of hooks, messages and images.

We've used this technique for many clients. After the results of an A/B test are tabulated, we take the winner (as the new A concept) and test another element (by developing a new B concept). We continue the process until we have optimized each element of the promotion (hook/headline, photos, graphics, copy and color).

This A/B testing process has become a standard for optimizing website page click-through and conversion rates. Google's Website Optimizer is a free tool that automatically splits your website traffic, sending half to page A, and half to page B. Then you analyze which page delivered the best results.

There are three primary benefits of A/B testing: 1) it measures actual behavior, 2) it generates revenue because you are distributing actual promotion, so A/B testing rarely ends up being an expense, and 3) you can use the results to optimize all of your promotion, not just the mail piece or webpage used in the A/B test.

As an example: when one copy point or feature beats out another in a direct mail A/B test, you could use that knowledge to strengthen a product sheet. When one photo beats out another on a webpage A/B test, you could use the best photo in your newspaper advertising.

Tip: It is important in A/B testing to change only one variable per test to isolate the element that made the difference. In other words, you would never test two different headlines and two different images in the same test.

Tracking Your Results

John Wanamaker, a 19th century entrepreneur, said, "I know that half of my advertising is wasted, I just don't know which half." Tracking your marketing activity may sound like an obvious practice, yet few small businesses develop and consistently use a solid tracking system.

> "However beautiful the strategy, you
> should occasionally look at the results."
>
> *Winston Churchill,*
> *British Prime Minister*

At the least, your tracking system should be designed to capture how every prospect and customer found you (which channel brought them to you). Ideally, your tracking system would also capture as much contact information as feasible. However, while that is doable in some industries it is not in others.

For example, if you sell business to business (B2B) it is not difficult to collect and enter information about a prospect into a customer relationship management (CRM) database. But if you are in retail, capturing contact information can be more difficult. Can you imagine if Starbucks tried to capture contact information at their drive-through windows? They'd go out of business.

Ways of collecting customer and prospect information include comment cards, a sweepstakes, or an incentive. When I bought my BlackBerry I was happy to fill out a comment card because of a $100 rebate.

The critical two steps in tracking are: 1) source where your leads are coming from, and 2) enter that information into a database. If you do not have a CRM system, I recommend setting up a simple spreadsheet to enter and tabulate the results based on sales. Your system needs to be easy to use for your staff or it will be difficult to maintain. If you have staff, make sure to include them when developing a user-friendly tracking system.

Review your results at regular intervals, no less than monthly. Based on your tracking information, continually re-optimize your promotional mix by canceling the underperforming channels and reallocating those freed up resources to channels that are more cost effective. This process will improve the overall performance of your promotion portfolio.

The key to success is to ask every prospect and every first-time customer how they found you. Help your team collect this source information by providing them with a list of all channels you are using for your promotion.

Tip: A common answer to the "how did you find us" question is a family member, friend or associate. When you hear that response, ask who gave the referral, so you can thank them.

"WOW!" Factor

The reason my phone rings is that companies want to optimize the results of their marketing activities, and most who call assume a new customer acquisition strategy is their best bet. But after conducting our client discovery process, we often recommend other ways for them to optimize their results that are more effective and less expensive.

One way that some businesses often overlook involves increasing the lifetime-market-value of their existing customers. While the most common tactics for doing this include re-selling, side-selling, or up-selling, the method I am about to illustrate has nothing to do with sales and everything to do with service. It's called the "WOW!" factor.

There is a saying in the car business that the sales department sells the first car, and the service department sells the second. This holds true in every industry. It doesn't matter how stellar your sales team or systems are, if a customer has a poor experience with a product or service after the sale, you probably won't get a second chance to earn their business, let alone a referral. Every business should deliver exceptional service after the sale.

Here is the takeaway. Merely meeting customer expectations does not generate a "viral buzz". After all, customers just expect their expectations will be met. Many studies have shown that when a brand has met a customer's expectation, that customer's rating of their experience is "neutral." Most customers who identify themselves as "satisfied" are in fact "neutral," not necessarily "loyal," and they rarely become "advocates."

If you want your customers to sing your praises, you have to do far better than meet their expectations. You literally need to "WOW" them. Think back to a time when you had a customer experience that actually made you say, "WOW!"

In the spring of 2003, my wife and I were talking with three landscape companies about a major project. But before we could select a contractor, doctors diagnosed a brain tumor (the size of a baseball) and I underwent immediate surgery. Needless to say, we had to make many changes, and canceling our landscape project was a no brainer (pardon the pun).

A few months into my recovery, my wife said to me, "WOW!" And then, "I can't believe what just happened!" The owner of Edmonds Landscaping, one of the three contractors, had called just to ask how I was doing. Not once did he mention landscaping, or our landscaping project. He was more concerned about our family. He was not a client or a friend, and the only way he knew us was through our prospective landscape project.

Seven years later we are still talking about that "WOW!" experience. Through my writing and speaking, I have shared that "WOW" story with hundreds of thousands of people.

Your company's "WOW!" factor will need to be big. Minor distinctions don't create advocates. The example I shared has more to do with company culture than a process or promotion. The most effective "WOW!" factors are served one customer at a time.

So bring your team together for a talk about what your company could do to "WOW!" your customers. If you're able to make your customers feel the way that landscaping company made me and my wife feel, you may not need to rely on a customer acquisition strategy ever again.

To truly optimize your results, pre-test and post-track your promotion, and "WOW!" your customers.

Step 8 Exercise Summary:

Pre-test all your advertising, publicity and sales promotion to optimize results by following this three-step process:

1 Develop your promotion concept, hooks, and key messages to present as mockups to a test group.

2 Recruit a customer advisory council from your best customers to acquire feedback on your promotion.

3 Optimize your promotion (messages) based on test group feedback, and optimize your channel (media) based on results.

Pre-Test Promotion

The purpose of pre-testing is to make sure your promotion concepts meet your objectives and create the desired results while reducing costs and increasing your return on investment.

☞ **Develop the Concept:**
Work with your media outlet (channel sales rep) to produce mockups (dummy ads or story boards) to present to your test group for feedback.

Determine what mockups you'll create:

_____

_____

☞ **Recruit Test Group:**
Your test group (focus group or consumer jury) can be recruited at no cost from existing customers who are invited to serve a one-year term on your Customer Advisory Council.

Develop your advisory council invitation list:

_____

_____

☞ **Optimize Your Promotion:**
Select the best promotion concepts based on your customer advisory council's feedback, and conduct A/B tests to further optimize your promotion (messages and images).

Determine your best concepts:

_____

Create the *Control* "A" concept:

_____

Make the change for the *Test* "B" concept:

_____

Based on your customer advisory council's feedback and the results of your A/B testing, optimize your promotion (messages and images) before launching your promotion.

Summary

"Reduce your plan to writing. The moment you complete
this, you will have definitely given concrete form
to the intangible desire."

Napoleon Hill,
Bestselling Author of Think and Grow Rich

As with any system, program or plan, documentation is crucial. Using the MAP System is no different than other programs in that regard. Writing down your plan and consistently reviewing it is essential to staying on track. Organize the results of the eight exercises sequentially into a document or folder, and you'll have a MAPS road guide to reference and to help you stay on course.

When meeting with prospective clients for the first time, one of my discovery questions is, "Do you have a marketing plan?" A few of them say, "Yes we do." Then I ask to see it and most of them reply, "It's filed away." Some aren't even sure where it is. I ask you, how does a "filed away" plan drive activity and accountability? Obviously, it doesn't (but somebody got to check off *marketing plan* as "completed" on their to-do list).

It accounts for why (and I can't tell you how many times) I've heard the complaint, "My marketing plan isn't working." Some of those plans were well prepared, so in those cases, the culprit was usually an absence of performance management and accountability. This perfectly illustrates the difference between "activity" (completing the plan) and "accomplishment" (implementing and tracking the actions detailed in the plan). Business owners and managers should keep their plans on their desks—not in file cabinets—and refer to them during management meetings.

We've all heard the adage, "Plan the work and then work the plan." The reason we keep hearing it is because it's true!

The MAPS Summary

☞ **Step 1:** _Finding Your Northstar_ is the trailhead of this journey. Don't skip this step as busy work, for it is the guidance system of the entire process. Every time you (or your team) grapple with an issue, idea or opportunity, run it through your mission statement, as the filter, and the answer will be clear.

☞ **Step 2:** _Analyzing Your Business_ involves conducting a market oriented SWOT Analysis. This will surface assets and liabilities that you'll want to leverage and mitigate. Shoring up and strengthening your operations are essential to growth, and will benefit every aspect of your business.

☞ **Step 3:** _Asking Your Customers_, as a means of collecting voice of the customer data, is the foundation of the MAP system. Having a better understanding of your best customers' preferences, perceptions, and experiences will lead you to making better business and marketing decisions.

☞ **Step 4:** _Studying Your Competitors_ is just as important because you cannot position your brand in a vacuum. Understanding the competitive landscape, and your key competitors' strengths and weaknesses, is necessary for developing a "distinctive" market position.

☞ **Step 5:** *Defining Your Niche* is the process of subdividing the market universe into segments, by profiling demographic (or corpographic if B2B) characteristics. The purpose is to concentrate your resources on a smaller, more responsive, and more profitable niche to create a bigger impact.

☞ **Step 6:** *Shaping Your Position,* based on your competencies, customer values, and competitor vulnerabilities, is what will distinguish your brand from key competitors in a manner that will be valued by your market niche. Your resulting unique value proposition will drive your promotion.

☞ **Step 7:** *Aligning Your Promotion* to your market position will ensure that the messaging and imaging are both meaningful and memorable. Aligning your well-positioned message to the right market, through the right channel, at the right time, will generate the best results.

☞ **Step 8:** *Optimizing Your Results,* based on pre-testing your promotion before you launch, and post-tracking the performance of each channel after you launch, will ultimately lead to more effective promotion, improvements in your return on investment, and the growth of your business.

Renewing Your MAPS

Since your business operates in a marketplace that is not static but dynamic and volatile, the MAP System is not a do-it-once-and-you're-done process. The market environment of constantly changing customers, competitors, government, technology and economy means your market analysis has a relatively short shelf life. For this reason, you will need to renew your data sets periodically.

I suggest that you conduct a SWOT analysis once a year, tied to your annual planning process. (You _do_ have an annual planning process for your business, right?) Also, staying abreast of what your key competitors are doing requires frequent monitoring. How often you need to renew the voice of your customer information is determined by your industry. Generally, customer research data rarely has a shelf life of more two years. However, if you are in an emerging or constantly changing industry, you will need to renew your information more frequently.

Undersell and Over Deliver

It's one thing to promise something, it's altogether another thing to deliver. The MAP System works remarkably well as a process to position a business (brand) for growth by accelerating sales. But after you position and promote your brand, it becomes a promise to customers, and you need to deliver on that promise.

> "While it may be true that the best advertising is word-of-mouth, never lose sight of the fact it also can be the worst advertising."
>
> _Jef I. Richards,_
> _Advertising Department Chairman_
> _University of Texas_

Delivering on your brand promise involves more than an attractive logo, catchy tagline and great promotion; it has more to do with the experience you create for your customers than anything else. When your customers talk about you, do they share their "WOW!" experiences or their "WORST!" experiences? With the rampant adoption of blogging and social media, one click can potentially make or break your business.

To assure your business "makes it" your brand promise should be promoted from the inside out. That means, the positioning and promotion process actually begins with your internal customers: staff and stakeholders. Remember this, if your internal customers don't fully understand and buy in to your brand promise, if they don't "get it," your external customers won't "experience it".

It's easier to define and promote a strong market position than it is to deliver on the customer expectations that are created by that position. My closing counsel is to undersell and over deliver—exceed on customer expectations.

If you go through and document all eight steps of this system—define and promote a market position based on the voice of your customers, and exceed their expectations—you will not only grow your business, you can became a leader in your industry.

Most important of all, always keep in mind that "**Your Opinion Doesn't Matter!** _It's Your Customer's Opinion That Counts._"

Special Offer to Help You Use MAPS Faster and Easier

Workbook

Because a new process is always easier to understand with visual aids, guidelines and tools, I am pleased to offer you a Workbook that includes worksheets for all of the "Step Exercises" described in the preceding pages.

Go to: YourOpinionDoesntMatter.com
Enter promo code: YODM for a 50% Savings
And Free Resources

Introduction:

According to the Small Business Administration only 34 percent of employer firms survive 10 years. Source: sba.gov/advo/stats/sbfaq.pdf 9/10/2010 (accessed 10/28/2010), page 15.

Webster's definition (2) of marketing. Source: Webster's New World College Dictionary (Fourth Edition © 2001), page 16.

Step 1:

Google's mission statement. Source: Google's company overview webpage - google.com/corporate (accessed 10/28/10), page 22.

FedEx mission statement Source: FedEx investor relations webpage - ir.fedex. com/documentdisplay.cfm?DocumentID=125 (accessed 10/28/2010), page 22.

Apple's mission statement. Source: Apples, investor relations FAQ webpage - phx.corporate-ir.net/phoenix.zhtml?c=107357&p=irol-faq#corpinfo2 (accessed 10/28/2010), page 23.

US bank specializes in SBA loans. This comment is based on US Bank's specialty division. Source: US Bank SBA Division - usbank.com/cgi_w/cfm/ small_business/sub_global/sba_loans_cu.cfm (accessed on 10/28/2010), page 24. The author acknowledges many other banks specialize in SBA lending, and that this is not necessarily a brand distinction.

Step 2:

9/11 attacks significantly increased American Flag sales. In the week after the [9/11] attacks, one of the nation's largest producers of American flags, Annin & Co. of Roseland, N.J., produced more than 50,000 flags – about 10 times the normal amount. Source: Staff writer at St. Petersburg Times, published September 8, 2002, page 37.

9/11 attaches devastated the airline industry. In testimony to Congress, Delta Airlines Chairman and CEO Leo Mullin estimated that the Sept. 11, 2001 attacks could cost the airline industry $18 billion to $33 billion in 2001. Source:

Hearing before the Committee on Transportation and Infrastructure, House of Representatives 107th Congress, first session on September 19, 2001, page 37.

The advent of micro processing put the kibosh on typewriter sales. The increasing dominance of personal computers and other electronic communication techniques have largely replaced typewriters in the United States. Source: en.wikipedia.org/wiki/Typewriter (accessed 10/28/2010), page 37.

Tale of two companies (Smith Corona and IBM). On July 5, 1995, the Smith Corona Corporation filed for bankruptcy protection in Delaware. Source: fundinguniverse.com/company-histories/Smith-Corona-Corp-Company-History.html. IBM introduced their 5150 on August 12, 1981. Source: en.wikipedia.org/wiki/IBM_Personal_Computer. IBM/clone PC market share in 1995 was 91%. Source: Ars Technica, December 14, 2005, By Jeremy Reimer - arstechnica.com/old/content/2005/12/total-share.ars/. IBM Fortune 500 listing in 1995 as #7. Source: Money/CNN.com (all URLs accessed on 10/28/2010), page 38.

Step 3:

Microsoft typically incentivizes with software. Source: My personal experience with a colleague who participated in a focus group to evaluate Microsoft Project in 1997, page 49.

Step 4:

Google Alert, a free tool from Google. Source: google.com/alerts (accessed on 10/28/2010), page 61.

Step 5:

Volvo sells less than 4 percent of what Toyota sells in terms of units. Source: Wall Street Journal/Market Data, September 2010 - online.wsj.com/mdc/public/page/2_3022-autosales.html (accessed on 10/28/2010), page 74.

Step 6:

With over 60 percent market share Heinz is the 800-pound gorilla in the catsup category. Source: Heinz 2004 Annual Report - wikinvest.com/stock/

H.J._Heinz_Company_(HNZ)#_note-2 (accessed on 10/28/2010), page 81.

Two Fortune 500 companies, Home Depot and Lowe's. Source: 2010 Fortune 500 list, ranked 29th and 42nd respectively - Money/CNN.com (accessed on 10/28/2010), page 82.

Bank of America was one of the first to distinguish itself by launching its mobile banking service. Source: Mobile Banking Catching On in US, Slowly. May 31, 2007 article in PCWorld - Bank of America Corp. in March launched mobile banking for 21 million online banking customers, allowing customers to use their cell phones and smart phones to check account balances, pay bills and transfer funds - pcworld.com/article/132456/mobile_banking_catching_on_in_us_slowly.html (accessed on 10/28/2010), page 83.

Dell changed the way consumers shop for computers, online instead of at a retail outlet. Dell started selling computers on Dell.com in 1996. Source: content.dell.com/us/en/corp/d/corp-comm/our-story-facts-about-dell.aspx (accessed on 10/28/2010), page 83.

UPS "What can 'Brown' do for you?" UPS unveils 'What can brown do for you?' ad campaign. Source: Business First, February 7, 2002 - bizjournals.com/louisville/stories/2002/02/04/daily35.html. Revenue share ratio over FedEx dropped from 1.56 in 2002 to 1.28 in 2010. Source: Fortune 500 list comparing revenues for both companies in 2002 and 2010 - Money/CNN.com (all URLs accessed on 10/28/2010), page 84.

GEICO was considered the fastest growing personal auto insurance company in the U.S., while State Farm, the category leader in 2000, had dropped from 15th to 34th on the Fortune 500 List (2000-2010). Source: GEICO Tops Ward's 50 Again, By Jeanny Hopper July 27, 2010 - autoquotenow.com/auto-insurance-news/headlines/geico-tops-wards-50-again-2-2729.php, and Fortune 500 list comparison of State Farm in 2000 and 2010 - Money/CNN.com (all URLs accessed on 10/28/2010), page 84.

GEICO's market share grew by 324 percent. Since Berkshire acquired control of Geico in 1996, its market share has increased from 2.5 percent to 8.1 percent - ecreditdaily.com/2010/03/geico-credit-cards-buffetts-painful-confession (accessed on 10/28/2010), page 88.

Step 7:

Hallmark knows that the bulk of their sales will occur based on holidays, so for Valentine's Day their timing is obvious. Source: Brandweek, January 26, 2004. One TV spot broke last week and the full schedule launches this week. Tag: "Hallmark Gold Crown - allbusiness.com/marketing-advertising/branding-brand-development/4688994-1.html (accessed on 10/28/2010), page 101.

GEICO, for example, is constantly advertising. Source: The Best Ad on Television, by Seth Stevenson, July 25, 2005. GEICO's "wall-to-wall" advertising - slate.com/id/2123285 (accessed 10/28/2010), page 102.

Nordstrom Half Yearly Sale. Source: Seattle PI Readers Blog by Tarah Perini, October 29, 2008. Plus, it only happens twice a year so make sure to stock up now! - blog.seattlepi.com/urbanfashionnetwork/archives/152845.asp (accessed on 10/29/2010), page 102.

They are not constantly advertising like GEICO, but they seem to be. Source: Gail Lavielle, a Wal-Mart spokeswoman, said the company wants to "have the very best resources [$578 million per year] to make sure we have consistent messaging, May 3, 2006 - msnbc.msn.com/id/12618548 (accessed on 10/28/2010), page 103.

Budweiser really ratchets up their spending level, during major sporting events. Source: Reuters, April 29, 2009. Anheuser-Busch historically has been the biggest U.S. corporate sponsor in the sports world and is still eager to promote itself through sports - forum.skyscraperpage.com/showthread.php?t=168512 (accessed on 10/28/2010), page 103.

Step 8:

Sometimes it does take a rocket scientist. Source: Absolute InBox, October 28, 2006 - absolutelyinbox.com (accessed on 10/28/2010), page 114.